THE Matters OF Her Heart

TAPESTRY COLLECTION

STORIES OF FAITH, TRIALS, AND TRIUMPHS
FROM SINGLE AND MARRIED WOMEN

FOREWORD WRITTEN BY
Geral Towne

COLLECTION WRITTEN BY
Ebony Alexandra, Satavia Hazley Austin, Dr. Kimberlee D. Bassa,
Dr. Katina Briscoe, Christin Burton, Dr. Kathlyn Spires Diaz, Brandi Epps,
Chrisdya S. Houston, Aveia Jones, Sherna L. Peterson, and Leondra Williams

The Matters of Her Heart Tapestry Collection
Stories of Faith, Trials, and Triumphs from Single and Married Women

Copyright © 2025

All rights reserved. This book or any portion thereof may not be reproduced or used in any manner whatsoever without the express written permission of the author except for the use of brief quotations in a book review.

ISBN 978-1-954595-39-2

Sparkle Publishing Company

www.sparklepublishing.net
Printed in the United States of America
San Diego, California

All biblical references are used from New American Standard Bible, New International Version, New Living Translation, and King James Version. ©

Table of Contents

Foreword 1

Dear Sis 3

When God Says, "Go Now!"
By Chrisdya S. Houston 5

A Perspective on Trusting in Times of Uncertainty
By Aveia Jones 15

The Thorn of Singleness
By Brandi Epps 25

Navigating the Valley
By Dr. Katina Briscoe 35

Deceit, Departure, and Deliverance
By Leondra Williams 43

Baby, You're Going to Be Ok
By Ebony Alexandra 53

Moving Forward Through Shattered Dreams
By Dr. Kathlyn Spires Diaz 61

The Past(or) Kid's Vision
By Christin Burton 71

Against the Odds
By Satavia Hazley Austin 79

A Diamond In the Rough
By Sherna L. Peterson 89

When You Just Don't Know What to Do
By Dr. Kimberlee D. Bassa 97

Pass Me the Fig Leaves Please
By Latriece M. Spires 103

Meet The Authors 111

Dedicated to our sisters who aren't yet ready to share their own stories. May they find comfort and strength in those who have gone before them.

Foreword

The first time I met Latriece was the year of 2001. She was my roommate freshman year of college at the University of Arkansas at Pine Bluff. That summer, when we were given our roommate assignment, she wrote me a letter introducing herself. To me, the letter seemed quite lengthy. I said to myself, "I hope she doesn't do a lot of talking all the time." In the letter it seemed she was a ball of energy. Finally meeting her in person, she was that and so much more. We have been friends ever since. She now has over 20 years of experience in education and leadership. She is an internationally award-winning author, life coach, business consultant, educator, motivator, and Christian woman. I know her best as my best friend. She created this Christian faith-based project, The Matters of Her Heart Tapestry Collection: Stories of Faith, Trials, and Triumphs from Single and Married Women. She is a co-author with eleven other women who share their stories from the heart. It was created to give these women a platform to share their journeys with others. In doing so, hopefully it will give hope and let others know that they're not alone in this thing called life. It will inspire and encourage you to not give up and keep the faith. Matthew 17:20 (KJV) states, "And Jesus said unto them, Because of your unbelief: for verily I say unto you, If ye have faith as a grain of mustard seed, ye shall say unto this mountain, Remove hence to yonder place; and it shall remove; and nothing shall be impossible unto you." This happens to be one of her favorite scriptures. So, sisters, hold on, keep the faith, and keep moving forward. Know that you are loved and that God loves you best.

Be blessed,
Geral Towne, MSN, APRN, FNP-C

Dear Sis,

You are not alone. Life can be challenging at times and it's essential that we are surrounded by the right people.

The Matters of Her Heart is a ministry that I founded with the sole purpose of creating a space for Christian women (both single and married) to join together to cultivate authentic, community while unpacking matters of the heart. We go through so much as women and it's important that we have the support from our communities.

I chose this book as a means to give my sisters in Christ a platform to share their stories, advance the Kingdom of God and to help other sisters, like you, along your Christian walk. My prayer is that as you see yourself in the text, that you will allow God to use your story for the advancement of His Kingdom.

Prepare your hearts to receive the wholesome transparency that awaits to meet your mind, body, and soul. May you receive all that He has in store for you. Be encouraged dear sis—God is still on the throne!

With your heart in mind,
Latriece M. Spires
Visionary Author

Chrisdya S. Houston

When God Says, "Go Now!"

By Chrisdya S. Houston

"'For I know the plans I have for you,' declares the Lord, 'plans to prosper you and not to harm you, plans to give you hope and a future.'" (Jeremiah 29:11 NIV)

My mother has repeated Jeremiah 29:11 to me since I was young, and she continues to do so even now. During difficult times, we often worry and wonder: *Is this supposed to be happening? Is this God-allowed? Am I destined to get through it? How—or if—will I make it to the other side?*

These were the exact worries and turmoils I began to feel as early as age five. Someone entered our lives who did not have good intentions—neither towards my mother nor me. One of my earliest memories of this unsettling time remains vivid. I was about five years old, sitting on the kitchen counter, when this man opened the refrigerator, pulled out a covered dish, and tried to make me eat cold okra straight from the fridge. It wasn't an act of humor, nor was it meant to nourish me. It was a calculated effort to intimidate a five-year-old girl—the pretty, brown-eyed girl in the patent leather Stride Rite shoes—who in every other circle was loved, cherished, doted upon, and treated as extraordinary.

To this day, I still do not eat okra.

God said that He *knows the thoughts that He thinks towards me…*

I'm not sure exactly when this man, who was in no way related to me, began hurting my mother and hitting me. But even as a child, I knew it was wrong, and I knew we had to escape. Thankfully, my mother knew it too, so we left—again and again.

We would flee to the home of one of my aunts or a friend. Yet, time after time, the abusive man—a minister, no less, who spent hot, Texas Saturday mornings evangelizing to bring people to Christ, who preached passionately on Sundays, but hurt us during the week and who arrogantly called himself "Greatness"—would track us down. He would show up at all hours, stalking and harassing our family members. I can still hear him screaming my mother's name across parking lots and driveways as he tried to force us out of whichever safe haven we had found.

When I think back on those times, I often find myself asking what thoughts God had toward us that He would "allow" these things to happen to my mother and me. I know that God loves us, yet when memories of those painful experiences resurface, I can't help but wonder: Why me? Why us? Why that kind of hurt?

In those moments of questioning, I sometimes weep for the parts of my childhood that I missed—the joys of childhood that I didn't get to fully experience. Still, I believe God turned that pain into purpose. Those experiences taught me how to slay monsters, how to speak up for myself and the mistreated, and how to rise to mountaintops despite the valley moments that life inevitably brings.

God said that He has *thoughts of peace, and not of evil (towards me)...*

Despite the many times my mother packed up and left to find refuge for us away from this clinger-on, and despite the countless visits from my aunts, who came to stay with us as buffers, offering what we now call a "side-eye," we remained in that situation far too long. God had thoughts of peace and not evil toward us, but "Greatness" had thoughts of chaos, evil, and manipulation. He wielded scripture as a weapon—using it to manipulate us into staying trapped with him. But thank God for His plans—plans of escape and exposure.

At eight years old, I was a quiet, studious, and intuitive third grader who excelled academically, even while hiding behind a veil of trauma. This trauma stemmed from a man whose actions I had learned to predict and whose presence I had grown to hate. Even at that young age, God spoke to me, giving me the courage to seek freedom and safety.

One day, "Greatness" left me home alone, threatening punishment upon his return if I moved from the spot he had dictated. It didn't matter whether I obeyed or not; he would punish me based on whatever he imagined I had done, with no proof and no mercy. I wrestled internally, and weighed my options. Should I stay and risk his wrath, or should I flee to freedom and safety?

I chose freedom and safety. Whatever the situation, I will always choose freedom and safety.

I opened the front door and knocked on the neighbor's door. The husband answered, and his wife was listening empathetically over his shoulder. I explained that there was an emergency, and I needed to get to my aunt's apartment. Even at eight, I knew exactly how to guide him to her place, which was in another part of town. Once we arrived, I thanked him, jumped out of the car, and ran up the stairs. Gasping for breath, I knocked on my aunt's door. When she opened it, I sobbed uncontrollably, and clung to her as I poured out everything that had been happening.

That moment marked the first steps toward ending the domestic abuse that had stolen my childhood happiness, joy, light-heartedness, trust, and even my childlike faith. Thank God for His plans—plans of escape and healing.

God said that He *plans to prosper me and not to harm me…*

God's intent is never to harm us. The human condition and free will lead to mistakes, turmoil, sin, and the hurt we all experience in some way or another. Most of the time, these painful memories are buried deep in my mind; other times, they surface at the forefront of my thoughts. I'll ask God, "Why did I have to go through that, Lord? Did You not love me? Was I not enough?" He always answers, "I am the One who got you through it. Yes, you are My daughter, and you are enough."

Through His grace, I've been able to grow past the palpable shock and hurt of those dark experiences, develop and nurture G.R.I.T.T., and encourage others who have faced difficult and hurtful experiences to not allow their pain to stifle their life's progression.

G.R.I.T.T. stands for Grace, Resilience, Intellect, Tenacity, and Talk. God can restore our wholeness and help us develop these traits as we work to rise above hurt, anger, sadness, and the absence of joy.

- Grace: Not only should we carry ourselves with grace, but we must also extend grace to others. However, grace does not mean tolerating harm. Be a person who fosters healing, not someone who perpetuates pain. And when others harm you, give yourself the grace to let them go and walk away from hurtful situations.

- Resilience: Resilience is our ability to bounce back from difficult times and keep going. God does not want us to remain down; our ability to rise is a testament to His power within us.

- Intellect: Be a reader, a learner, a thinker, and a doer. Cultivate discernment to distinguish between right and wrong, truth and falsehood, and God's voice from others. Critical thinking is vital. How often have we focused on surface details or blindly accepted what we were told, only to regret not digging deeper? Take the time to reflect, analyze, and understand before making decisions, taking action, or letting the wrong people into your life.

- Tenacity: This is the persistence and determination to achieve or complete something meaningful. What goal have you been putting off? Let today be the day you decide to move forward.

- Talk: Shining a light on hurt or problems is often the first step to healing. Consider how many harms could be avoided if we weren't a society steeped in keeping secrets. Find a safe and trustworthy source, and speak up to access the support and relief you need.

These characteristics were in my spirit as a child and have strengthened over the years, helping me succeed in my undergraduate and graduate studies, navigate my career and entrepreneurial life, build relationships, and nurture my bond with my loving mother.

Over the years, my mother and I have had salient conversations about what we've overcome. Together, we've prayed for the ability to forgive and to flourish beyond those dark times. God's love and guidance have been our anchor, enabling us to rise above and continue to grow.

God said that He *plans to give me hope and a future…*

We can have hopes and dreams, but only God truly knows what our lives will look like—from conception to the end. Life takes unexpected turns, descends into valleys, and soars to mountaintops we never anticipated or planned. No matter what we face, God wants us to know that He is here for us and that His plans are for us to have hope and a future. As an 8-year-old girl, I hoped to escape a harmful situation and envisioned a future that did not include being harmed. God spoke to me and said, "Go now." I listened in that very moment.

I listened then so I could become the woman who treasures a personal relationship with God and has a restored and unwavering faith in Him. I listened then so I could graduate from SMU with three Bachelor's degrees in just five years. I listened then so I could be the educator who prioritizes students' well-being and helps them build G.R.I.T.T. to face life's challenges. I listened then so I could use my voice to speak up when others cannot. I listened then so I could become a successful entrepreneur and inspire others to pursue their entrepreneurial dreams. I listened then to bring justice to myself and my mother, allowing us both to flourish in life. I listened then so I could help other survivors of domestic violence move beyond what was done to them, reminding them that God is always there, and wants them to be safe and free from harm. His desire is not just for us to survive but to thrive—a concept that I call "thrival!"

Prayer:

Dear God, we ask for Your forgiveness for any unconfessed sins and for any pain we may have caused others. Lord, we also ask that You open the doors of safety and freedom for anyone experiencing a domestic violence situation. Grant them the strength to develop G.R.I.T.T. as they leave that situation and transition into a phase of "thrival." We pray they emerge on the other side victorious, not as victims, and that they reach for the hope and future You have promised them.

Lord, we also pray that you will lead anyone who is an abuser to ask for Your forgiveness, to ask for the forgiveness of those they have harmed, to seek emotional help, and for the women and children that they are abusing to go now to safety and security without threat or interference.

In Your precious name, we pray. Amen.

Reflection:

1. What do you need to ask, say, or do to reach a place of forgiveness?

   _____

   _____

   _____

2. Which elements of G.R.I.T.T. are currently your strongest? Which elements do you need to strengthen?

   _____

   _____

   _____

3. How could you use the elements of G.R.I.T.T. in a situation you currently face?

   _____

   _____

   _____

"I'd rather take a chance on myself instead of continuing to support a narrative I no longer find value."

-Latriece M. Spires

Aveia Jones

A Perspective on Trusting in Times of Uncertainty

By Aveia Jones

"So do not worry, saying, 'What shall we eat? or What shall we drink?' or 'What shall we wear?' For the pagans run after all these things, and your heavenly Father knows that you need them. But seek first his kingdom and his righteousness, and all these things will be given to you as well. Therefore do not worry about tomorrow, for tomorrow will worry about itself. Each day has enough trouble of its own." (Matthew 6:31-34 NIV)

When I heard the words, "I am officially diagnosing you with anxiety," my heart didn't drop the way I thought it would. I was actually relieved. Before, I thought I couldn't give in to anxiety or fear because God doesn't want me to worry. What I came to realize was that I had allowed external circumstances to influence the voice within. That diagnosis became the catalyst I needed to induce a long-overdue change. It unleashed a determination I had been searching for—a determination I knew was inside. It gave me permission to say no and walk away from anyone or anything that did not align with who God says I am.

This chapter is dedicated to all those who find themselves shackled by corporate America, while also being unmarried and childless, and facing the challenge of caring for aging or ill parents. When our ambitions and abilities are viewed as threats by those who wield immediate power over our livelihoods and impose their perceptions on our realities, we must remember that immediate power is not ultimate power. Only God holds ultimate power. We must adjust our lens and adopt a perspective that maintains alignment with God's will.

For me, I was at a critical juncture in my life and career, with serious ambitions in real estate and personal desires as well. I had just purchased my first home, a decision God very clearly guided me to make. At the time, it felt as though God was placing me in an environment that would nurture my dreams and allow me to explore the dating world. I would witness construction and development come to life daily, motivating me to build my dreams and bring the family life I desire to reality. This journey was a faith walk in itself, as I learned the great lesson found in Psalm 24—everything belongs to God.

During the purchase process, I faced financial uncertainty. I prayed and shared my heart with the Lord, and it was as if He responded, "It's already done." Shortly after, I received a message from the sales team informing me of an overlooked incentive toward closing costs or a rate buy-down. Just like that, Jesus paid it all! I witnessed His provision in a miraculous way.

Fast forward to closing day—it went smoothly. Three months later, I learned the true purpose of this experience. My mother was diagnosed with breast cancer. To convince her to complete a mammogram, I persuaded her to visit my doctors in the Metroplex. Little did I know, this would be a turning point, teaching me lessons of perseverance, survival, and battles on multiple fronts. I realized my relocation was about creating a setting for healing and restoration—not only for my parents' health but also for my faith perspective.

A Perspective on Trusting in Times of Uncertainty

As you can see, I'm no stranger to trusting God and taking leaps of faith. I've never shied away from hard work or challenges, but my experience in corporate America forced me to think deeply from a spiritual perspective. Had I allowed these jobs and their paychecks to become idols? The Word warns us about this. I realized the ease of earning a paycheck had caused me to 'give God a break.' Let me pause here—I know it sounds crazy, but it's real. I had also avoided the rollercoaster of dating because I was financially independent. Meanwhile, my spirit was in turmoil, yearning for a connection to the Father and seeking deeper meaning in my daily work and fulfillment of a family of my own.

At the same time, I found everyone on the receiving end of my efforts to be ungrateful, audacious, and illogical—both professionally and personally. I was trying to care for my parents, yet I was criticized, discouraged, and faced tension, stress, and discomfort at every turn. These feelings persisted because I delayed surrendering all to God.

How do I surrender? In my limited perspective, I thought I was capable and competent, and God had other children who truly needed His help. However, the Word clearly says God cares for all His children and instructs us to cast all our cares on Him. In doing so, I learned that perspective comes from many angles. I not only needed to pray for myself but also to intercede for those who didn't know how to pray for themselves, even those who mistreated me. The more I prayed for others from their perspective of need, the more I saw God working in unimaginable ways. Those miserable workdays stopped intimidating me. I knew I was doing my best, even when resources and time were scarce.

I shifted my focus to working for God, not for man. I stopped fearing financial loss and worrying about caring for my parents. Remarkably, the finances and resources never stopped, and my ability to care for my parents continued with the help of family, friends, and even strangers. Fear and worry were relinquished.

Fast forward to today—I am living in a whole new world. My parents are both cancer-free and healing more each day. Professionally, I am thriving. God provided an opportunity for me to use my skills in an environment that supports me just as I am. I have leadership that believes in my abilities, recognizes my growth areas, and is excited to guide me toward my professional goals. In addition, I have also gained clarity on my needs and desires in my next relationship. I know God will deliver the right man at the right time. After what felt like an eternity of struggle and stress, God suddenly turned my situation around, bringing this phase of my testimony full circle.

Now, I would like to share with you the heart of the matter—actionable steps and perspectives to help anyone experiencing similar struggles with doubt and fear when earthly support feels limited and heart's desires seem impossible:

- Seek Guidance from God - "Trust in the Lord with all your heart and lean not on your own understanding; in all your ways submit to him, and he will make your paths straight." (Proverbs 3:5-6)

  When overwhelmed, pause to pray and seek God's wisdom, as He promises to guide us when we trust Him. Ask Him to reveal what truly matters and how to proceed.

A Perspective on Trusting in Times of Uncertainty

- Rest in His Presence - "Come to me, all you who are weary and burdened, and I will give you rest." (Matthew 11:28)

  God invites us to bring our burdens to Him. Rest isn't just physical; it's spiritual and emotional. Spending time in prayer, worship, and reflection replenishes our souls and restores perspective.

- Acknowledge Your Limitations and Rely on God's Strength - "But he said to me, 'My grace is sufficient for you, for my power is made perfect in weakness.' Therefore I will boast all the more gladly about my weaknesses, so that Christ's power may rest on me." (2 Corinthians 12:9)

  Admit when you're at your limit. Depend on God's strength rather than striving on your own. He often uses our weaknesses to display His power.

- Prioritize - "'Martha, Martha,' the Lord answered, 'you are worried and upset about many things, but few things are needed—or indeed only one.'" (Luke 10:41–42)

  Jesus reminds Martha to focus on what's truly important. Similarly, identify tasks that align with God's priorities for you.

- Ask for Help - "Carry each other's burdens, and in this way you will fulfill the law of Christ." (Galatians 6:2)

  Don't hesitate to ask for help. God often provides support through community, friends, family, or colleagues.

- Take it Step by Step - "Therefore do not worry about tomorrow, for tomorrow will worry about itself. Each day has enough trouble of its own." (Matthew 6:34)

Break tasks into manageable steps. Focus on today's responsibilities without being consumed by the weight of future tasks.

- Reflect on God's Faithfulness - "Cast your cares on the Lord and he will sustain you; he will never let the righteous be shaken." (Psalm 55:22)

Look back on how God has sustained you in the past to renew your faith and confidence in Him.

- Work as Worship - "Whatever you do, work at it with all your heart, as working for the Lord, not for human masters." (Colossians 3:23)

Shift your perspective. When work is done for God's glory, it becomes meaningful, and burdens feel lighter.

By following these principles, you can find restoration, balance, and strength in God, even when life feels overwhelming.

Prayer:

I come to You today with a heart full of gratitude for all that You have done and all that You will do. On behalf of every sister striving to achieve greatness, even as the weight of the world rests on her shoulders and life's demands feel overwhelming, I ask that You remind her she is safe in Your arms. Assure her that Your promises will be fulfilled in her life.

Lord, we acknowledge the moments of despair, anxiety, and deep sorrow we experience as we wait for the fulfillment of Your promises to give us the desires of our hearts. I ask that You

A Perspective on Trusting in Times of Uncertainty

grant her the strength to surrender and cast all her anxieties upon You. Your Word in Philippians 4:6-7 reminds us:

"Do not be anxious about anything, but in every situation, by prayer and petition, with thanksgiving, present your requests to God. And the peace of God, which transcends all understanding, will guard your hearts and your minds in Christ Jesus."

Help us to reflect continually on Your goodness, trusting that blessings will come as we surrender our cares to You. In the precious name of Jesus, we pray. Amen.

Reflection:

Now that I have shared a part of my story with you, I hope you can relate and find inspiration to implement the steps I used to overcome anxiety, doubts, and fears. You are worthy of the time and care it takes to nurture your well-being and step into the fullness of your purpose.

1. Are you taking time to renew your mind with the Word of God?

   _____

   _____

   _____

2. In what areas are you holding on to burdens with your own limited strength?

   _____

   _____

   _____

3. Are you seeing others the way Christ sees us so that you may offer empathy and intercede on their behalf, especially when they are not doing the same for you?

   _____

   _____

   _____

4. What can you surrender to God right now that would totally change your life for the better?

   _____

   _____

   _____

> "When the tide subsides, everything is uncovered at the surface."
>
> —Latriece M. Spires

Brandi Epps

The Thorn of Singleness

By Brandi Epps

"If I wanted to boast, I would be no fool in doing so, because I would be telling the truth. But I won't do it, because I don't want anyone to give me credit beyond what they can see in my life or hear in my message, even though I have received such wonderful revelations from God. So to keep me from becoming proud, I was given a thorn in my flesh, a messenger from Satan to torment me and keep me from becoming proud. Three different times I begged the Lord to take it away. Each time he said, 'My grace is all you need. My power works best in weakness.' So now I am glad to boast about my weaknesses, so that the power of Christ can work through me. That's why I take pleasure in my weaknesses, and in the insults, hardships, persecutions, and troubles that I suffer for Christ. For when I am weak, then I am strong." (2 Corinthians 12:6-10 NLT)

Opening

The rose has always held a quiet allure for me—simple yet endlessly captivating. One afternoon, as I wandered through the floral section in search of a fresh bouquet, I found myself lingering, drawn into the rose's hidden depths. I admired its soft, layered petals, traced the elegant arc of its stem, and then felt the sudden, sharp sting of its thorns. Roses enchant with their fragrance and vivid petals, but their thorns reveal a deeper complexity—a reminder that life, especially single life, is a tapestry of beauty and pain interwoven.

Biblically, Paul understood something about the interplay of beauty and pain through his experience with *thorns*. In 2 Corinthians 12:7, he describes his *thorn in the flesh* as a persistent struggle meant to keep him humble and reliant on God. As I gazed at the rose's thorns, connecting their symbolism to Paul's metaphorical *thorn*, a realization began to take shape. Just as Paul's thorn served as an ongoing challenge, could singleness, too, be a kind of *thorn*—a challenge we may wish to escape but one that serves a divine purpose?

What if singleness is God's way of keeping us grounded, drawing us closer to Him, and preparing us for a relationship or marriage that will not only endure but flourish? Perhaps, like the rose, singleness carries within it a hidden beauty.

Faith and Trials

After an extended period of singleness, it's natural to start questioning what it is about ourselves that has kept us in this season. As a single woman of four years, I've wrestled with persistent doubts: Am I somehow unworthy of the relationship or marriage I desire? Do I still have inner work to do? Am I perhaps not as ready as I think I am? Is there truly a shortage of quality men out there?

Left unchecked, these thoughts can easily consume us, filling our minds with so much noise that we miss the gentle voice of God speaking in our singleness. When life becomes too noisy, I know it's time to be still—to step away from the sights and sounds of social media, the distractions of dating apps, and everything else vying for my attention. In the quiet, as I tuned my heart to hear from God, His answer to my questions about being single left me stunned. In an unmistakably clear tone, He whispered, "Brandi, your singleness is the only way for Me to keep you at bay with Me."

The phrase "keep at bay" means to control something or prevent it from becoming a problem. I wondered: Was God saying dating was causing me unwarranted problems? If so, what kind? As I sat with Him, understanding began to unfold. Fellow singles, I invite you to lean in—because I've been the gatekeeper of this message long enough, and God has called me to share it.

What I've come to realize as a spiritually mature single is this: My struggles in dating were never about my unworthiness, readiness, or inner work, nor were they caused by a lack of quality men. That mindset only traps us in endless cycles of questioning, blame, and disappointment. The real issue? It's our difficulty in keeping God first—prioritizing Him before, during, and even after He brings someone into our lives.

In 1 Corinthians 7:32-35, Paul provides valuable insights for unmarried men and women:

> "I want you to be free from the concerns of this life. An unmarried man can spend his time doing the Lord's work and thinking how to please him. But a married man has to think about his earthly responsibilities and how to please his wife. His interests are divided. In the same way, a woman who is no longer married or has never been married can be devoted to the Lord and holy in body and in spirit. But a married woman has to think about her earthly responsibilities and how to please her husband. I am saying this for your benefit, not to place restrictions on you. I want you to do whatever will help you serve the Lord best, with as few distractions as possible."

This passage reminded me that singleness is a season in which we have the most uninterrupted time with God. In marriage, our attention is naturally divided as we fulfill the needs of a spouse. But when we, as singles, struggle to keep God first—neglecting to seek Him, study His Word, or remain holy in body and spirit—we risk being redirected back to Him in unexpected ways. This often happens when we idolize those we're dating or in relationships with, placing them in a position only God should hold.

Take my own experience. During seasons of singleness, I've undoubtedly felt lonely, undervalued, and longed for companionship. Yet, I've also experienced some of my most focused and disciplined times with God—as though He equipped me with a superpower to endure! In these seasons, I rise early to read His Word, pray throughout the day, study Scripture, and consume biblically-based content. These moments embody the principles outlined in 1 Corinthians.

But when God aligns His will with mine and sends a saved, tall, educated, well-dressed, bearded gentleman into my life (if you know me, you know!), my spiritual disciplines often slip away. My time and energy shift toward meeting his needs, creating space between God and me. Deuteronomy 4:23-24 reminds us the Lord our God is a jealous God who forbids us from making idols of any shape or form—even those saved, tall, educated, well-dressed, bearded ones.

So how does God respond when I've placed someone above Him? He ALLOWS that person to slip from my grasp, grabs hold of His sharpest *thorn*, and proverbially wedges it into my side to bring me back to Him. The pain? Unbearable.

Yet, returning to singleness and starting over is often the only way God can help us see the bigger picture He has in mind. Matthew 6:33 paints this vividly: "Seek the Kingdom of God above all else (including those gentlemen/women and the traits you love so much about them), and live righteously (led by the Holy Spirit, not your fickle emotions), and he will give you everything you need."

As painful as it's been—and certainly not what I would have chosen for myself—it was exactly what I needed. God knew the restoration of our relationship required it.

Triumph

In times like these, we can be grateful for a God who loves us so deeply that He refuses to let us remain on shaky ground. His love reaches us in the midst of our struggles, extending the grace we need to bring us back to our senses. This reminds me of Paul and his *thorn in the flesh*.

In 2 Corinthians 12:7-10, Paul shares that to keep him from becoming proud, he was given a *thorn in his flesh*. On three occasions, he pleaded with God to remove it, but God's response was filled with love and humility. Each time Paul asked, God replied, "My grace is all you need. My power works best in weakness." Isn't it just like God to meet us in our weakness and bring us back to clarity when we're losing our way?

Paul's acknowledgment of God's sovereignty in these verses leads him to embrace his struggles, even finding joy in his weaknesses, insults, hardships, persecutions, and troubles for the sake of Christ. In the moments Paul feels weak, God's strength is magnified. Let that be an encouragement to you, dear brother or sister.

Your singleness may feel like a painful *thorn in your side*—something you desperately wish to escape. But consider the hidden blessings it brings:

- It keeps you humble.
- It allows you to remain close to God and His Word.
- It provides uninterrupted time with God, time that will inevitably be shared in a relationship or marriage.
- It affords you the opportunity to intentionally keep God in His rightful place as the head of your life.
- It prevents you from becoming overly prideful, self-centered, or boastful.
- It demonstrates the power of fully relying on God, His grace, and His strength.

The spiritually immature Brandi once saw singleness as a punishment for her personal and relational mistakes. But the spiritually mature Brandi now sees this *thorn* of singleness as a necessity—not just to keep her close to God but to equip her with the spiritual foundations essential to becoming a Proverbs 31 woman and a wife in the making!

Prayer:

Lord, thank You for the thorn of singleness in my life. I now understand that its sting was never meant to harm me but to draw me closer to You. Help me remain steadfast in Your presence, Lord. Strengthen me to prioritize time with You, discipline myself to stay rooted in Your Word, and grow into the best version of myself—for Your glory and for my future mate.

In moments when the weight of singleness shakes me to my core, remind me that Your grace is sufficient, providing all I need to endure the tests and trials of this season. Remind me, too, that Your power is made perfect in my weakness. Singleness no longer holds authority over me, my choices, or my peace. Instead, let it become the foundation that prepares me to walk boldly into a Godly relationship and marriage, firmly grounded in You.

In Jesus' holy and majestic name. Amen.

Reflection:

1. How is the thorn of singleness currently impacting your intimacy and relationship with God?

   _____

   _____

   _____

2. What has God revealed to you about your current priorities, and what actionable steps are you ready to take in response?

   _____

   _____

   _____

3. How can the assurance that God's grace is sufficient, and that His power is made perfect in your weakness, inspire you to embrace your singleness with a renewed perspective moving forward?

   _____

   _____

   _____

"Oh, I'm just someone who recognized her potential and decided to do something with it."

—Latriece M. Spires

Dr. Katina Briscoe

Navigating the Valley

By Dr. Katina Briscoe

"The Lord is my shepherd; I shall not want. He maketh me to lie down in green pastures: he leadeth me beside the still waters. He restoreth my soul: he leadeth me in the paths of righteousness for his name's sake. Yea, though I walk through the valley of the shadow of death, I will fear no evil: for thou art with me; thy rod and thy staff they comfort me. Thou preparest a table before me in the presence of mine enemies: thou anointest my head with oil; my cup runneth over. Surely goodness and mercy shall follow me all the days of my life: and I will dwell in the house of the Lord for ever." (Psalm 23:1-6 KJV)

As women, we all face trials—whether publicly or privately, challenges are inevitable. Sometimes, our misery becomes our ministry. My story could be the key that unlocks someone else's prison. Our shared experiences as women create common ground. Looking back, there's nothing I could have done differently—except, perhaps, to have avoided the situation altogether.

That's why Psalm 23 holds such deep meaning for me. It begins with images of green pastures and still, restful waters. But we often want to skip over the valley experience, avoiding pain, discomfort, or moments of discontent. We rush ahead, eager to reach the table God has prepared for us, without realizing that Jesus is in the valley, waiting. In that place of struggle, He uses our experiences to teach us profound lessons about gratitude and trust in Him.

Sometimes, we stray from the path God has set before us. With the best of intentions, we follow the wrong ideas, trying to make distractions align with His will. In doing so, we take a detour—making a left turn right into life's valleys. But even in the midst of those difficult seasons, we are never alone. He is always with us.

October 2, 1991

I was in my bedroom, just as I had been the last time I heard my daddy sing. It was an early fall morning, and I could smell the change in the air. My sisters were getting ready for school, and I was feeling some type of way. Everything irritated me, and I couldn't figure out why. I felt uncomfortable and anxious. I didn't know whether to lay down, stand up, or stick my foot out and trip one of my sisters. Either way, I knew I was going to do something soon.

As I stood up, my eyes landed on the calendar, and that's when it hit me: the date. My daddy had been gone for nine years. I was 18 and I remember thinking, *A lot can happen in nine years.* At that moment, it felt like the baby I was carrying slid off a shelf in my stomach—that's the best way I can describe it. He was in my birth canal, and it was not a good feeling. That's when the pain started. I glanced at the calendar again. He was due tomorrow. He was coming, but I was determined it wouldn't be today. I made up my mind right then: this baby was going to have to wait.

The house grew quiet once my sisters left for school. For the first time that morning, I was alone. I didn't tell anyone what I was feeling. The person who had promised me everything—things I had no right to expect—was nowhere to be found. Mama had been right again. "You have a baby, and it's all yours," she'd said. Pushing those thoughts aside, I spent the next few hours sitting in a chair. Eventually, the pain stopped. When everyone came home that afternoon, I was fine. I got up, moved around, and didn't say a word about the pain I'd endured all day. October 3, 1991, came and went.

October 4, 1991

I spent the early morning hours sitting on the edge of my bed, watching old movies. Before I realized it, I'd been up all night and couldn't get comfortable. By 6 a.m., the house was alive with movement, but I couldn't stand up. My back hurt so badly it felt like it might break in half. Mama walked in and asked, "Girl, are you hurting?" Mothers just seem to know. True to my oppositional nature, I replied, "Nope." But inside, I was barely holding it together.

By then, I couldn't deny it anymore: I was about to have a baby. I sat down, trying to recall everything I'd been told to do—pack a bag (which I hadn't done) and time the contractions (which I'd been ignoring all night). Then I realized: I didn't have time. I washed my hands, looked at Mama, and said, "I'm in labor."

Later that morning, my nurse practitioner confirmed what I already knew. "Are you ready to have this baby?" she asked. "As ready as I'll ever be," I replied. The pain was beyond description. Walking helped for a while, but eventually, even that became impossible.

Wave after wave of pain hit me, and I labored through the night. Mama stayed home; she said her nerves weren't built for this. A friend drove me to the hospital. Lying in the backseat, I groaned softly with every contraction. My friend's sister, who was driving, joked, "If the police stop this car, you'd better act like that baby is on its way out!"

I labored alone. No one came to hold my hand or tell me it would be all right. I had no epidural, and I felt every ounce of pain. Sometime after 7 a.m. on October 5, I was taken to delivery. The urge to push was uncontrollable, and when I tried to stop, I felt my flesh tear. The doctor arrived as my baby was born. When I finally heard his cry, relief took over. It took forty stitches to repair the tear.

When they placed him in my arms, I looked at his tiny face and thought, *What am I going to do?* My tears fell onto his soft skin. Who would guide me? How would I take care of him? What would I name him? I thought about my daddy. He would've been angry at me, but I also knew he would've loved his grandson. My tears now represented all the things my daddy never got to see.

In that moment, not only did I turn to the Lord, but I also gave my baby to Him. My son's name means wisdom, intelligence, and that God is gracious. I believed He would forgive me, provide, and guide us. I didn't recognize it at the time, but I felt empowered. I started asking the nurses questions and learning how to care for my baby.

It took time for me to heal emotionally. Postpartum depression hit hard, and in our community, mental health wasn't something we talked about. I didn't have words for what I was feeling. I was trying to be a mother, work, and figure out what had just happened to me. I felt lower than low, like I didn't deserve happiness. Life went on for everyone else, but I was just trying to survive.

Now, all these years later, I look back with gratitude. God brought me through. He made a way when I couldn't see one. I share this story through the eyes of an 18-year-old girl who gave birth alone, entrusting strangers with her most vulnerable moments. What I felt most after all the fear and pain was resolve. I was determined to give my baby the best I could, knowing God would provide what I couldn't. My sisters in Christ, whatever trials you are facing, there is an answer in the Word of God for you.

Prayer:

Dear Heavenly Father,

I thank and praise You for being the Lord of my life. Today, I lift up the sisters who are reading this prayer, asking that You cover them with Your love and grace. May Your will be done in their lives, for the safest place we can be is in Your will.

Lord, Your Word promises that even when we walk through the valley, You are with us. I ask that You continue to guide us as we navigate these valleys, reminding us that there is a table prepared for us on the other side.

Father, I thank You in advance because no season of loss, loneliness, or uncertainty is beyond Your care. Be a constant reminder to my sisters that they are never alone. Lord, give them the strength to release their burdens to You and trust You fully, leaving their worries at Your feet. In Jesus' name. Amen.

Reflection:

1. Reflect on a time when you faced a significant challenge at a young age. What would you share from that experience to help someone else?

   _____

   _____

   _____

2. In what ways can we effectively mentor young women today, given the challenges they face?

   _____

   _____

   _____

3. Are there any fears or uncertainties you experience when working with young women in this age group?

   _____

   _____

   _____

"Pivot the plan, not your purpose."

-Latriece M. Spires

Leondra Williams

Deceit, Departure, and Deliverance

By Leondra Williams

"The righteous cry, and the Lord heareth, and delivereth them out of all of their troubles." (Psalms 34:17 KJV)

"Not that I speak in respect of want: for I have learned, in whatsoever state I am, therewith to be content." (Philippians 4:11 KJV)

The Opening

One day, the mountain that is in front of you will be so far behind you, it will barely be visible in the distance. But the person you become in learning to get over it? That will stay with you forever. And that is the point of the mountain. – Brianna Wiest

Faith and Trials

Have you ever stayed in a seasonal position longer than you were meant to? Whew, Sister, I have—and I'm guilty as charged! Guilty of lingering in spaces I was only meant to pass through, long past my exit date, and it caused me significant discomfort. I've been guilty of this in both my personal and professional life, but in this chapter, my focus is on the personal.

Let me start by introducing myself. I am a Bible-believing Christian who loves the Lord deeply. I'm also a divorced, single mother of three incredible children: ages 23, 17, and 10. My children are among the greatest joys of my life. They are my "why." Whenever

I've felt like giving up, quitting has never been an option because I strive to model resilience and purpose for them.

I'm an educator and a servant at heart in every role I fulfill. I've often been described as someone who cares too much—overpromising myself to the point of exhaustion, trying to be everything for everyone, and too often forgetting to take care of myself.

Overstaying in Seasonal Spaces

In my personal life, I've been guilty of overstaying my seasonal position in relationships. Whether it was a serious dating relationship, a marriage, or a friendship, I've remained in spaces well beyond the clear signs of a season's change—the ones purposefully designed to be my exit. I've often reflected on why, despite having every sign to leave, I doubted myself and couldn't seem to take the necessary steps to make the timely exit God had prepared for me. Why did I continue striving for relational harmony when chaos was all around me? Why did I stay when deceit had become the norm?

Deceit. You know, that purposeful falsehood Merriam-Webster defines so plainly. The answer is simple: I wasn't truly trusting God.

"And why call ye me, Lord, Lord,

and do not the things which I say?" (Luke 6:46)

What happens when we fail to trust God? Maybe not always the same for everyone, but for me, I know this: when God saw that I wouldn't leave on my own, He made sure I had no other option but to exit. Have you ever heard someone say, "Don't make God make you leave?" Yes, that's exactly what I'm talking about.

When I reached the point where I didn't know how I'd provide daily necessities for my children or myself, I cried out to God and leaned completely on the One who holds tomorrow.

"Many things about tomorrow I don't seem to understand, but I know who holds tomorrow, and I know who holds my hand." – Ira Stanphill

In that moment, no matter how dire things seemed, my trust rested solely in the Heavenly Father. I learned that trusting God is easy to say but often harder to do. I specifically recall God working in my life, requiring not only my trust but also my obedience. I realized that obedience is the byproduct of trust—you cannot obey if you don't surrender and truly trust God.

Through trusting and obeying God, I experienced spiritual, physical, social, emotional, and financial realignment. But realignment didn't happen overnight. It took years to heal from the trauma of deceit and heartbreak that led to my ultimate exit. That exit wasn't easy. Afterward, I endured a multi-year storm that included therapy, surrounding myself with the right people, credit recovery, strict budgeting, and, most importantly, resting in God's unfailing love. I made the choice to obey and trust Him no matter what life looked like.

Everything I went through became one of the greatest learning experiences of my life. Why? Because I would face deceit again. But this time, because I was God-led, I had the skills to recognize it, navigate it through Christ, act promptly, exit on schedule, and stand gracefully.

Before I stopped merely saying I trusted God and truly surrendered, I was like the lame man sitting at the gate called Beautiful (Acts 3:1-9). I remained in a storm longer than necessary because I hadn't fully surrendered. But when I finally let God lead, He gave me access to resources and gifts that helped me heal and rebuild. Therapy guided me to surround myself with the "Peters and Johns" in my life. I left the darkness, embraced God's blessings, and intentionally used the resources He provided—credit recovery, strict budgeting, and, most of all, His unwavering love. Before I knew it, my life reflected Acts 3:10:

"And they knew that it was he which sat for alms at the Beautiful gate of the temple: and they were filled with wonder and amazement at that which had happened unto him."

Nobody understood how I managed:

- To keep food on the table for my children
- To clothe my children and myself
- To maintain my peace of mind
- To buy a new vehicle
- To receive a call from a stranger offering to sell me a home under market value at $30,000; nonetheless, I got it for $28,000 in a neighborhood that blessed my family
- To advance in my career
- To see God handle my enemies while I remained still

Trust and obedience opened doors that had always been there but were inaccessible until I surrendered. They unlocked the door to *WIN*. People often say, "It's my winning season." But here's the truth: winning isn't seasonal when you trust and obey God—it's a daily reality. God's goodness isn't limited to what we deserve. As Matthew 5:45 reminds us:

"That ye may be the children of your Father which is in heaven: for he maketh his sun to rise on the evil and on the good, and sendeth rain on the just and on the unjust."

We will all have good and challenging days, but because God grants us another day, we always win. Trust and obedience have made my good days outweigh the bad and brought me back to my Savior when I tried to handle things on my own.

Triumph

Sister, do you want to know what it truly looked and felt like when I started to trust God and walk in obedience? It was a lot like Philippians 4:11:

"Not that I speak in respect of want: for I have learned,

in whatsoever state I am, therewith to be content."

When I reflect on that verse, two key things the Apostle Paul said stand out: our season and our response.

Our season is the "whatsoever state":

- Heartbreak
- Death
- Financial distress
- Job woes
- Children gone astray

Our response is contentment. But not man's contentment, which the world defines as mere satisfaction. I'm talking about spiritual contentment—seeking after Christ alone!

Spiritual contentment is a mindset that causes all other things to fade away. It is simple obedience to God. I'm living proof that spiritual contentment removes discontentment, transforms your actions, and changes your spiritual response to your "whatsoever" season. Debbie Hinkle once shared that Spiritual contentment reminds us that "God is just as good in the valley as He is on the mountaintop." Spiritual contentment will give you that perspective.

A content woman knows that God is the author and finisher of her story. A content woman understands that He is both the giver and the taker. A content woman chooses unspeakable joy over temporary happiness. A content woman submits, surrenders, and gives everything over to God—no matter what!

Contentment is the result of obedience to God. Obedience requires submission, surrender, and preparation for whatever God leads us to. This means obedience is the secret ingredient for what comes next in our lives. It is the key that unlocks the door to the next level. Sister, I had to make the decision that when the temptations of the world seemed faster than God's elevation, I would choose to obey Him.

Obedience unlocks doors and prepares us for "whatsoever." Contentment, in turn, provides rest in God. Whether you are in your "whatsoever" season, standing on the mountain, or walking through the valley, nothing can separate you from doing God's will when you are spiritually content. His children, those who trust and obey Him, can find rest—even when nothing else makes sense.

Prayer:

Dear God,

I thank You for the woman of God reading this text today. I ask that You be the lifter of her head and grant her the strength to reflect honestly on her journey. Help her to acknowledge where she is, how she arrived at this place, and whether she is content with being here. Reveal to her if she has missed an exit You provided or if she is in need of one now.

Teach her to call on You, lean on You, trust You, and obey You. Show her the blessings and benefits of serving You through trust and obedience. Let her know that You are all she needs. Remind Your daughter of Your promise in Isaiah 1:19: "If ye be willing and obedient, ye shall eat the good of the land."

Thank You, Jesus. Amen.

Reflection:

Sister, take a moment to reflect on your journey. Read the questions below and answer them with complete honesty. Talk to God and let Him guide your thoughts and steps.

1. Where are you in life?

   _____

   _____

   _____

2. How did you get here?

   _____

   _____

   _____

3. Are you truly okay with where you are?

   _____

   _____

   _____

4. If not, have you missed the exit God provided for you?

   _____

   _____

   _____

"Everybody doesn't deserve premium access to you. Card accordingly."

—Latriece M. Spires

Ebony Alexandra

Baby, You're Going to Be Ok

By Ebony Alexandra

"'Never will I leave you; never will I forsake you.'" (Hebrews 13:5 NIV)

Difficult situations and challenges in life often test the depth of a person's beliefs and convictions, pushing them to their limits. These moments reveal the strength of one's faith in the face of adversity. Trusting that God will always be present and never abandon you, no matter how tough life becomes, is essential.

My mother suffered from a long-term illness, so seeing her go in and out of the hospital had become our norm. I had become accustomed to her being hospitalized for a week or two, getting better, and then coming home. She always came home. But this time felt different. As she was leaving in the ambulance, I remember looking at her thinking: mommy looks really sick, really weak, and really tired. And in that moment, I really didn't want her to go. I didn't want her to leave our home, but I had no say or choice. She needed to go so that she could get better and come home.

Growing up, summer was my favorite time of the year! I loved spending my days with friends and family, roaming the neighborhood, taking long walks around the city with my best friend, and trying to make it home before curfew. I cherished those moments when I could simply be a kid and not worry about adult responsibilities, which too often became my reality. Circumstances beyond my control forced me to grow up quickly. With a sickly mother, I often had to step into adult roles at home because she was physically unable to manage. It became my responsibility to do the grocery shopping, keep the house clean, and take care of her when she couldn't take care of herself.

My mother didn't like being alone, so she often wanted me to stay home with her. Most of the time, I obeyed, but I felt restricted—like I was being punished or missing out. I would beg her to let me leave, promising to check on her soon, and eventually, she would give in. Still, I resented seeing her in such a vulnerable state. Watching her struggle to care for herself or for me was heartbreaking. It took a toll on me. I craved normalcy and would escape to spend time with friends, trying to feel like a regular teenager, even though nothing about my life felt normal.

One early July morning, my cousin called and asked me to come over. Any chance to escape, I would take. I told my mother I was going, but she didn't want me to leave. I promised her I wouldn't be gone long and that I'd come back to check on her. She reluctantly let me go. I spent the day with my cousins, but that evening, my two older sisters came to pick me up. My mother had called them because she wasn't feeling well. They were upset with me for being gone so long and told me I could never do that again.

When we got home, my mother was incredibly weak and struggling to breathe. I felt terrible for leaving her when she had begged me to stay. We called an ambulance, and she was taken back to the hospital. But this time felt different. I could see it. I wasn't sure she would be coming home.

After hours in the emergency room, she was admitted, and we were told to return in the morning. When my sisters and I visited her the next day, she looked frail and weak—so much so that I was afraid to touch her. My mom told us she was tired. She didn't want to live like that anymore. She told my sisters she wanted to sign a DNR (Do Not Resuscitate) order and begged us not to fight her decision. I was in complete shock. She was telling us she didn't want to live, and there was nothing I could do. My sisters honored her wishes and signed the papers. She told us to leave and get our other sister so she could see her. I remember not wanting to leave. Somehow, I knew this was it. I held her hand and said, "You can't leave me. I don't want to live with my sisters." She looked at me and said, "You're my last pea in the pod, baby. You're going to be okay."

Those were the last words my mother ever said to me. She slipped into unconsciousness and passed away the next day. At just fifteen years old, I became a motherless child. The little girl who already felt like her life wasn't normal now had no mother. What do I do now?

Losing my mother had a profound impact on my life. I felt lost, hurt, and angry—angry at the world, angry at my mother for leaving me, and angry at God for taking her. I questioned Him: Why would You let this happen to me? Was I not deserving of my mother's love and guidance through life? My faith was tested, and I felt abandoned. I told myself that I had no choice but to grow up.

I found myself trying to figure out life on my own. I was looking for love in the wrong places and trusting people I shouldn't have. I caused a lot of self-inflicted pain and carried a burden of regret that weighed heavily on my shoulders. I lacked the wisdom to navigate the complexities of relationships and the challenges of growing up. I made mistakes that left scars, both emotionally and mentally, and often felt lost in a world that seemed too big and unforgiving.

Like me, many of us are facing loss and pain, carrying burdens that feel too heavy to bear. But in the midst of our struggles, we must learn to trust God, knowing that He sees our tears, hears our prayers, and walks with us through every storm. I had to learn to trust God when there was no one else. Trusting Him doesn't mean the pain disappears instantly, but it means we can rest in His promise that He will never leave us nor forsake us. It means believing that even in our darkest moments, He is our light, guiding us toward healing and restoration.

When we place our trust in God, we begin to see that our pain has a purpose and that He can use even the hardest seasons of our lives to strengthen us and shape our character. He can take what was meant to harm us and turn it into something beautiful—a testimony of His faithfulness and power. Trusting God allows us to exchange our fear for peace, our sorrow for joy, and our brokenness for wholeness.

Along with God, my mother's last words to me, "Baby, you're going to be okay," have carried me through my darkest moments. No matter what challenges I've faced, her reassurance has proven true. Even in her absence, I feel her guiding and protecting me from above. My mother's love and God's unwavering presence have been with me every step of the way. Proverbs 3:5-6 reminds me of the peace that comes from trusting in God's plan, even when I don't fully understand it. His wisdom is greater than ours, and He never abandoned me—not even in my deepest pain.

By leaning into His love and acknowledging Him, He continues to direct my path toward healing, purpose, and deeper faith. My life is a testimony to His faithfulness and the unbreakable bond of love I still feel from my mom. The trials we face are not the end of our story—they are the refining fire shaping us into something extraordinary. God sees our struggles and stands by His promise: "When you pass through the waters, I will be with you; and when you pass through the rivers, they will not sweep over you. When you walk through the fire, you will not be burned" (Isaiah 43:2).

Though the road may be rough, know this: God is working all things for your good (Romans 8:28). Your pain has a purpose. Your challenges have meaning. Trust in His timing and His plan, even when the path ahead is unclear. "Consider it pure joy, my brothers and sisters, whenever you face trials of many kinds, because you know that the testing of your faith produces perseverance" (James 1:2-3).

Trust and know this: You will be okay.

Prayer:

My Prayer to My Sisters Weathering Life's Storms

Dear Heavenly Father,

I lift up my sisters in Christ who are walking through storms they never expected. Lord, You see their pain, their struggles, and their weariness. Remind them that they are not alone, for You are their refuge and strength, a very present help in trouble (Psalm 46:1).

Father, calm the raging seas around them and speak peace into their hearts. Grant them the courage to trust in You when the path feels uncertain. Your Word assures us that "those who hope in the Lord will renew their strength; they will soar on wings like eagles" (Isaiah 40:31). Renew their strength today, Lord.

Fill them with Your unfailing love, remind them of Your promises, and give them the patience to wait for Your perfect timing. Let them feel the comfort of Your arms around them, guiding and sustaining them through every challenge.

Lord, turn their trials into testimonies and their pain into purpose. Let their faith shine brighter than the storms they face, and may Your joy overflow in their hearts, even in the midst of hardship.

In Jesus' name, we declare that no storm will overcome them because You are their anchor. Bless them, protect them, and carry them through with Your mighty hand. Amen.

Reflection:

1. How has trusting God during your storms shaped and transformed your faith journey?

   _____

   _____

   _____

2. In what ways has God already provided for you or strengthened you throughout this storm?

   _____

   _____

   _____

3. Are there any burdens or fears you need to lay at the feet of Jesus today?

   _____

   _____

   _____

Dr. Kathlyn Spires Diaz

Moving Forward Through Shattered Dreams

By Dr. Kathlyn Spires Diaz

"Forgetting what is behind and straining toward what is ahead, I press on toward the goal to win the prize for which God has called me heavenward in Christ Jesus." (Philippians 3:13-14 NIV)

As a young girl, I remember dreaming of being happily married, owning a home, and serving in the community with my husband. My hope was to be married to a godly man, like my father, who loved his wife, family, and devoted himself to serving the Lord. This dream was inspired by my parents' example, who demonstrated the importance of loving God as key to a successful life. My parents practiced biblical values and instructed their children on how to love and serve others. From these principles, I dreamed of a Christian marriage like my parents and I believed my marriage would create wholeness and divine purpose in my life. As an adult, I centered my goals, career, and education around the hope of partnering with someone who would love, support, and grow with me. Unfortunately, my decisions led to two unsuccessful marriages and feelings of depression and self doubt. This journey began at the age of twenty and continued for forty years of "wandering through the wilderness." My story illustrates my faith in Jesus Christ, through bad decisions and life's trials and triumphs. This chapter highlights critical years living as a single mother, completing my doctorate degree, subsequently marrying into a different culture, experiencing familial isolation, and finding hope. My aim is that you will be inspired by reading my story, learn from my mistakes, seek the Lord for your purpose, and become all HE created you to be.

Singlemotherhood

We learn through life's challenges. Often our journey is like a roller-coaster ride with ups, downs, and unpredictable outcomes. I entered into my first marriage at the age of twenty, where my ups and downs began: from the birth of my son, to a divorce eleven years later, to suddenly becoming a single mother. My first husband often left my son and I alone to seek his fortune and indulge in outside relationships. As a result of his infidelity, we divorced. My heart was crushed, fragmented, and fearful of the responsibility of paying all the bills. The odds were stacked up against me! I knew I was not qualified to handle the challenges of raising a Black male alone. I prayed fervently for answers and God provided them. God rescued me! The Holy Spirit lovingly convicted me, helped me to forgive my former spouse, and embrace my future. From His loving grace, He sent ministering angels in the form of my family, church, and the local Black community. My prayer for financial stability was answered by working with my sister-in-law who is a Certified Public Accountant. She met with me to review my budget and to my dismay, we discovered that after paying all my bills, I would only have $20 left between paydays. I remember my Sis telling me, "Kat, you may be at the bottom now, but there is ONLY one way to go, AND THAT'S UP!" Eventually, my turnaround happened by following my budget plan and paying my tithes and bills on time. God used human vessels such as my father and four brothers who became mentors and helped provide the male role models and personal accountability my son needed. They were the examples of positive, successful Black men in his life and I embraced the love and the wisdom they imparted unto my son. I was grateful for strong family ties, a safe space for healing, and restoration. Additionally, my church and the Black community helped foster growth in my faith and historical context of how African Americans excel in times of adversity. My worries and fears about single motherhood diminished, and I began dreaming again. As I spent more time with the Holy Spirit, He opened my heart to my passion to improve my high school Spanish skills, travel abroad, and serve in my local community.

The Lord opened doors for me to develop my Spanish-speaking abilities in the community as a volunteer and through mission work in Latin America. For many years, I volunteered as an ESL instructor and later went back to school. Upon completion of my master's degree, my friend and mentor (Dr. Regina Smith) encouraged me to continue my scholarly pursuits. I applied to the University of Arizona's Second Language Acquisition and Teaching Doctoral Program. To my surprise, I was accepted and offered a one-year full scholarship. In the years that followed, I received a Graduate Student Teaching Fellowship in the Spanish department's Basic Language Program. The Lord exceeded my expectations granting me favor, opened doors, and I walked through them.

Completing My Doctorate Degree

The doors opened for me to attend the University of Arizona in Tucson, Arizona. In spite of Tucson's extreme heat, I was excited about the opportunity of higher education. Weeks later, after settling in and "coming down from the mountaintop," reality hit: I had moved far away from home. Fears and doubts overshadowed my thinking. Two weeks into the fall semester, I received feedback from some professors that my writing skills were not adequate. I wondered whether or not I was cut-out for graduate school. I became anxious and could not retain new information. As a result, I failed my first exam. I thought: God must have made a mistake, because learning should be much easier, right? I did not understand that my failure was an opportunity for God to turn it out for my good (Romans 8:28). He purged me and revealed areas of pride and lack of humility. The Holy Spirit revealed I could do nothing outside of Him. I repented, humbled myself, and the Lord showed next steps to overcome.

The first step: The Holy Spirit led me to an on-campus Writing Skills Center, and I connected to a tutor. The second step: I met with the professor who gave me an F on my exam. At first, I felt tension in the air as I entered her office. I told her that I was not there to question my grade, but to learn from my mistakes. Immediately, her countenance changed. We talked about my strengths and interests and discovered that I was a visual and auditory learner. During study time, I applied this learning, passed the next exam with an A, and received an A for my semester grade. God blessed me continually and my successes increased.

Marrying Into a Different Culture

Ultimately, my greatest success was graduating with a doctorate degree in good standing. The glory goes to God for His faithfulness, grace, and love. However, despite all my successes in education, I still had a void of not having a relationship with someone. I pondered the validity of a "prophetic word" given to me many years earlier. The prophetic word spoken at my grandmother's funeral was by a respected minister who said I would remarry to a godly Hispanic man serving together as ministers. In my mind, I objected to marrying a "Macho" man, closed that door, and focused on my future career.

Career driven, I was focused. Feeling conflicted, lonely and isolated, I searched and found a church with a diverse body of believers who spoke English and Spanish. I felt comfortable worshiping in Spanish and soon got involved in singing on a Praise Team. I felt God's calling to minister through song. One year later, a woman from the congregation inquired if I would be interested in meeting her brother who resided in Mexico. At first, I refused and told her that I was only interested in my studies at the University. As the conversation continued, she convinced me to meet him, highlighting our common interests in serving the Lord and helping others. Six months later, we fell in love and the next year married. I did not realize at the time that I would also be marrying deep cultural traditions and influences that would shape how we saw the world and how we interacted with each other. There was an unyielding pressure to conform to the Mexican way. His mother, the matriarch of the family, did not like that her son married a Black woman and she negatively influenced and controlled him. Unfortunately, after fifteen years of marriage, we divorced. Once again, my dreams were shattered into unrecognizable pieces that only God could put back together, then heal, and create beauty from ashes.

Isolation

Isolation, whether voluntary or forced, is unhealthy and can promote damaging mental illnesses. As a believer, I knew that I had to forgive my former spouse and his family for taking advantage of my good nature. But honestly, I was unable to do that. I remembered years of feeling isolated as though I was an outlier or a second class member of his family, never fully measuring up to their expectations, no matter how hard I tried. Inwardly, I became depressed, gained weight, and lost my sense of purpose. My parents' values taught me to love everyone; however, the only family I had in Arizona did not reciprocate the embrace. During the divorce, my four brothers encouraged me to move back to Portland. First, I had to find employment and literally start all over again financially. After submitting several job applications and attending many interviews, I accepted a position in the public sector. My mind was focused on returning home and being with my family. At the time, I was unaware how depression and anxiety had affected my mental state and overall health.

Depression can come on suddenly, incrementally, or in a combination of the two. In the winter of 2024, an ice storm in Portland helped me identify how I suppressed my emotions and how my health suffered from it. I cried out to the Lord for help, and as He always does, He heard my cry! I prayed to God to help me forgive myself and all my transgressors. The Holy Spirit taught me that forgiveness is a process. Daily, I commit to pray for those who have hurt me and He heals and restores me. Additionally, the Holy Spirit identified what I needed to do to restore my emotional well-being and reconnect to the community. The Holy Spirit led me to join a gym and consistently work out with a trainer. This physical activity not only strengthens my muscles and circulation, but also I'm beginning to see improvement in my overall mindset. Also, I began to understand that I needed to lovingly distance myself from those who did not want to change their bad habits and trust God to bring the right people into my life.

Hope

Now in my early 60s and after all I've been through, I'm finally winning! I'm abiding in the knowledge that God still has a plan for my life. I'm no longer languishing in a state of depression and shame. I'm experiencing the Lord's peace and His joy. And I have the God-given hope of receiving much, much more of the same.

I'm consistently in the gym three days a week, aiding in my mental health while getting my physical health together, too. God has blessed me with the best and highest paying job I've ever had. I get to work independently, largely from home, and I feel that in a small way, I'm making a difference in my community. I'm a living testimony that God is true to His Word. He will never leave me or forsake me and that same promise applies to you!

Prayer:

Holy Spirit, I pray that those who read my story will be encouraged to follow You closer than ever before. I pray, Lord Jesus, that You will give your daughters divine hope and peace that no matter what they're facing, they will know that You are the answer and that You are their hope! In Jesus' name I pray. Amen.

Reflection:

1. What is God's will for your life?

   _____

   _____

   _____

2. Do you know your purpose?

   _____

   _____

   _____

3. How do you allow the Holy Spirit to teach and guide you in your daily walk?

   _____

   _____

   _____

"You don't owe anyone an explanation for doing things differently, you're on assignment."

-Latriece M. Spires

Christin Burton

The Past(or) Kid's Vision

By Christin Burton

"So do not fear, for I am with you; do not be dismayed, for I am your God. I will strengthen you and help you; I will uphold you with my righteous right hand." (Isaiah 41:10 NIV)

The Opening

I woke up and turned to my left. The person lying next to me was unrecognizable, even though we had been together for about a year. I was still sore from the argument we had a week prior. But on this day, I woke up—not just physically, but spiritually. It felt as though God had tapped me on the shoulder and, despite my stubbornness, showed me exactly what I was investing my time in.

The Body

Her hair no longer glowed as it once did. Her skin, once flawless and golden brown, now appeared old, dry, and cold to the touch. Her eyes were sunken, and her breathing was labored. As I stared at the person lying next to me, her scent smelled of yesterday—stale. Yesterday had been the catalyst for the change that needed to happen in my life. When she shifted in the bed, I jumped. Her irritation at being disturbed forced me to lay back down. As her hands touched me, I became stiff, knowing that the same hands that had once shown affection were now weapons that tore me down.

I had always believed that loyalty and love were proven by enduring pain and hardships without turning my back on anyone. I was in a lesbian relationship, and I can admit that I loved this individual more than I loved myself. Unintentionally, I had placed her above God—before being a mother, a daughter, a person, my sobriety, a sibling, and most importantly, a child of God. My past hurts and traumas had created a revolving door of relationships that ended in abuse, addiction, loss, and grief. But that day, I realized something had to change.

As I planned my escape, I faced a harsh reality: she had both sets of keys. However, I managed to get my daughter out of the house and to school. This day marked the turning point of my life. It revealed not only who this person truly was but also the toxic cycles I had created for myself over the years and the roots of those cycles. I reached out to my boss and explained that I couldn't come to work because I was being physically abused. My boss reassured me and suggested a safe phrase: "Are you coming into work tomorrow?" If I said yes, it meant to call 911; if I said no, I was safe. My phone was taken shortly after that conversation, but her concern gave me some comfort.

In that moment, I prayed: "God, if you get me out of this, I will never go back." I realized that I had allowed this mistreatment—not just of myself but also of my children, family, and friends. I made it my mission to clean house and never return to that place of despair. As the day progressed, I tried to de-escalate the situation, buying time until I could pick up my daughter from my dad's house at 3:30 pm. I clung to the memory of the night before when, in a rare moment of stillness, I had grabbed my Bible. The kids were asleep, and the house was silent and peaceful. In the midst of my tears—tears of embarrassment, disgust, and desperation—I opened the Bible and found clarity in Isaiah 41:10: "So do not fear, for I am with you; do not be dismayed, for I am your God. I will strengthen you and help you; I will uphold you with my righteous right hand." Those words gave me the reassurance I needed. For the first time in a long time, I felt God's presence and surrendered fully to Him.

As the day continued, the physical and verbal abuse persisted. When it came time to pick up my daughter, she insisted on accompanying me. During the drive, I reflected on the life I had allowed myself to live—the compromises, the pain, and the addictions. I repeated to myself, "I surrender." Isaiah 41:10 became my anchor, reminding me that with God by my side, I could overcome anything.

When I arrived at my father's house, I was broken but could not show it. I hugged my oldest daughter and whispered for her to tell my dad to call 911 in ten minutes. I insisted that both of them stay with him. Once I returned home, I refused to get out of the car. The police arrived and escorted her off my property. That moment was my breakthrough—a turning point where I chose to seek Christ, pursue sobriety, and never look back.

Facing my fears was terrifying. I had to confront my childhood traumas as one of five children, a pastor's daughter raised in the church. I had judged my father deeply for not addressing his own wounds and for being two different people—one at church and another at home. This judgment blurred my understanding of religion and spirituality, merging the two into a single flawed perception. Holding onto the negative aspects of my parents blinded me to the fact that I was repeating their mistakes in my adult life.

As I put my faith in Christ, a pivotal test came when this same individual resurfaced, offering me drugs. I stood firm in my decision and went into complete silence, cutting off all contact. A quote from James Baldwin resonated deeply with me: "Not everything that is faced can be changed, but nothing can be changed until it is faced." He wrote an article in The New York Times on January 14, 1962 called "As Much Truth as One Can Bear." I had to face the pain, abuse, and mistakes, but I also had to take accountability for my part in it all.

What ultimately saved me was immersing myself in the Word of God and rebuilding myself mentally, emotionally, and spiritually. I repaired broken relationships and established boundaries, something I had always felt guilty about before. As I read deeper into Scripture, I realized many of the teachings ingrained in me as a child—to stay silent, to endure, to keep family secrets—were not aligned with God's truth. Jesus didn't call us to silence; He called us to speak, to be authentic, and to tell our stories.

The most beautiful moments in my life have been the intimate ones with Christ. In the stillness of my home, I felt His presence, guiding and consoling me. My greatest feat was starting my podcast, Get Out of Dodge. I recorded the first episode on my birthday, June 6, 2024, despite battling COVID. The support from my family and the respect I gained for my sobriety and transformation were overwhelming.

If I could tell any woman one thing, it would be this: Put Christ first in everything you do. It's okay to feel fear, but act in faith anyway. Surrender your self-doubt and your past. You don't have to be perfect to come to Christ. What you see as imperfection is the testimony that will inspire someone else. Share your story—someone out there needs to hear it.

Prayer:

Heavenly Father,

I come before You with a humble heart. First and foremost, Lord, thank You! Thank You for the gift of life, new perspectives, experience, and wisdom.

Lord, I ask that You use me as a vessel to pour into my sisters. I lift up all the women who encounter these words, praying they spark something within them—a longing to draw closer to You. I pray that any pain, turmoil, or chaos weighing on their spirits or minds be silenced so they can hear Your voice clearly.

Father, please allow them to feel Your presence, heal from their wounds, and grow into the women You've called them to be. Surround them with people who will pour into them with love, wisdom, and encouragement so that they, in turn, can pour into others.

Lord, I ask that You free their hearts, minds, and souls from any bondage, breaking every chain that holds them back. Let Your grace and mercy intervene in their lives, guiding and sustaining each one of them. Amen.

Reflection:

1. What are the core issues that cause the choices you make?

   _____
   _____
   _____

2. How do you allow Christ to lead you in trials and tribulations?

   _____
   _____
   _____

3. How has your life changed once you surrendered to Christ?

   _____
   _____
   _____

4. When did you know God was working in your situation?

   _____
   _____
   _____

> "Trusting God hits different in this season.
> He hasn't changed, I have."
>
> —Latriece M. Spires

Satavia Hazley Austin

Against the Odds

By Satavia Hazley Austin

"And we know that God causes everything to work together for the good of those who love God and are called according to his purpose for them." (Romans 8:28 NLT)

God orchestrates all things—even the painful moments—into a masterpiece for our ultimate good. Trust that God is always at work, even when we cannot see the full picture. Life can be unpredictable, often feeling like a roller coaster of unfavorable events. Sometimes, it simply makes no sense. The Bible is filled with stories of real, flawed people navigating less-than-ideal circumstances. This doesn't diminish Christianity; instead, it demonstrates the humanity of its followers.

You can have faith and still feel sadness. Even Jesus expressed anger and sorrow yet remained steadfast, fulfilling His mission on the cross. Your faith does not diminish because of these emotions. After all, Jesus wept. Although faith serves as an anchor, the waters can still feel deep. As the Word says, you will reap if you faint not (Galatians 6:9). James 1:2-4 states "when troubles of any kind come your way, consider it an opportunity for great joy. For you know that when your faith is tested, your endurance has a chance to grow. So let it grow, for when your endurance is fully developed, you will be perfect and complete, needing nothing."

According to Pew Research Center, only 1 in 4 parents living with a child in the U.S. today are married. The likelihood of a child being raised in an unmarried household is significant, given the fluidity of modern family dynamics. Over the past 50 years, there has been a decline in marriage rates and an increase in births outside of marriage. This marks a dramatic shift from half a century ago, when fewer than 1 in 10 parents living with their children were unmarried.

Consider me as an example: I was born to two college students—an 18-year-old young woman and a 19-year-old young man. Both came from middle-class families, but neither resided in a shared home with both parents. My young mother, in one of the world's largest cities, was navigating life 200 miles away from her family with a new baby. I was the first grandchild, deeply loved by both sides of my family. Despite their bright futures, the demands of early parenthood delayed their dreams. My father dropped out of college to enter the workforce, while my mother continued to pursue higher education and work.

Like many young couples, their relationship eventually faltered. According to the Wall Street Journal, two-thirds of couples experience a decline in relationship quality within three years of a child's birth. Similarly, my parents—although at one time were very much in love—agreed to separate and co-parent. That was very disappointing and hard for all of us. Having to rotate weekends and holidays between my parents was challenging. Leaving my mother alone for some holidays (because her family was not in town) and not being with the two people I loved the most was extremely hard. I imagine it was very hard for them as well.

I became a part of the 40% of U.S. children born to unwed mothers, with 63% of African American children raised in single-parent households. Oftentimes, these households live at or below the poverty level. Raising a child is a non-stop, challenging and expensive task, but doing it with one parent in the home can result in missed opportunities, lack of supervision and resources, and added stress. These statistics reflect a systemic issue, not a justification. However, attitudes toward marriage and single parent households have evolved, influenced by greater opportunities for women. The women in my life embodied the modern woman—independent, career-focused, and economically self-sufficient. The shift allowed for different life choices compared to previous generations.

Research shows that many women now delay marriage, focusing first on careers, independence, personal fulfillment, and financial freedom. My mother exemplified this trajectory. She earned her doctorate with the highest honors, married after I went to college but divorced after 17 years of marriage. My father, though never married, also achieved fulfillment and financial freedom through a strong work ethic.

I grew up witnessing the values of education, independence, and hard work. I graduated magna cum laude, became a debutante, competed in pageants, performed in theater, and pursued higher education. By age 26, I had purchased a home, acquired an investment property, and became an entrepreneur. By 30, I held a corporate leadership role while running a successful small business.

After professional achievements, I turned to personal fulfillment, seeking to become a wife and mother. While I had seen colleagues marry and build families, this path was unfamiliar to me. Raised to value education and independence, I hadn't dreamed of weddings or white picket fences—my dreams revolved around success and self-sufficiency. Guidance on marriage and relationships had not been fostered or taught by the women I looked up to and admired.

Relying on God, prayer, and counsel, I began this new journey. Despite my efforts, my first son was born out of wedlock. Like me, my son was deeply loved by both sides of the family. His father and I got engaged; however, the relationship still didn't survive. I was devastated but determined to give my son the stability and love I longed for. My son became my world, teaching me first hand that professional success alone couldn't sustain me for the role of his mother. Through complete surrender, I allowed God to lead me. He promised: when you hold a righteous course, He will erase the memory of your heartache, rewrite your story, fill you with joy, and place you above reproach (Psalm 119).

God fulfilled His promise. I regained strength and confidence, and He blessed me with a Godly man who loved my son and me wholeheartedly. We attended the same church and met formally after service at a popular brunch restaurant. Our love story, rooted in friendship and divine destiny, led to a beautiful wedding surrounded by family and friends. We now have two sons who bring us immense joy. My oldest son has a relationship with his father and is a great big brother. In a miraculous twist, my parents reunited after over 40 years apart. Our holidays together and family outings truly make my heart smile.

My life has been a journey, often unpredictable and impractical. As Creator, Author, and Finisher, God sees the beginning, middle, and end. Many times, I've had to reframe challenges as opportunities for growth, trusting God to get the glory in all things. I laughed once when I heard "count it all joy," because all is not joyous. In hindsight, I have discovered that there is joy when you stay the course and maintain a believer's point of view using the Bible as your roadmap when looking for direction in the life God has planned for you. Be encouraged that you can be all that God created you to be no matter your past experiences, societal trends, or family history. Understanding God's desire for wives and husbands is crucial to the family unit and legacy you create.

What does scripture say about a Godly wife?

- She brings fruitfulness and joy into the household. (Psalm 128:3)
- She shows deference to his Godly leadership. (Ephesians 5:33)
- She is wise and diligent in creating a peaceful and God-centered atmosphere. (Proverbs 14:1)
- She approaches life with wisdom, fear of the Lord, and grace. (Proverbs 31:25)
- She willingly aligns herself under Godly authority, trusting in God's design. (Ephesians 5:22)
- She brings honor to him and uplifts his leadership. (Proverbs 12:4)

- She guards her words and brings healing through her speech. (Proverbs 31:26)
- She intercedes for her husband and family with unwavering faith. (James 5:16)
- Her ultimate loyalty and submission are to God, which reflects in her marriage. (Proverbs 31:30)

What does scripture say about a Godly husband?

- He takes responsibility for the spiritual direction of his home. (Joshua 24:15)
- He sacrifices and serves her selflessly. (Ephesians 5:25)
- He speaks life and truth into her, ensuring she grows in her faith. (Ephesians 5:25-26)
- He works diligently to meet the physical, emotional, and spiritual needs of his family. (1 Timothy 5:8)
- He treats her with care, recognizing her value and honoring her as a co-heir in Christ. (1 Peter 3:7)
- He stands firm in his faith and is unwavering in the face of adversity. (1 Corinthians 16:13)
- He leads with grace, modeling the forgiveness Christ has shown him. (Colossians 3:13)
- He seeks God's guidance in all decisions. (Proverbs 3:5-6)
- He intercedes for his wife and children continually, seeking God's will for their lives. (1 Thessalonians 5:17)

These scriptures not only serve as a roadmap for a Godly union, but can also apply to all seasons of your life. As you continue to grow in Christ, His wisdom and love will equip you to navigate every challenge in order to experience the fullness of His promises.

Prayer:

In the name of Jesus, I stand firm against every societal statistic, ancestral bond, and inherited pattern that does not align with the Word of God. According to 1 Peter 5:10, in His kindness, God called me to share in His eternal glory by means of Christ Jesus. After I have suffered a little while, He will restore, support, and strengthen me, and place me on a firm foundation.

God is my hedge and my example. His Word is a light unto my feet, guiding my path. Anything I lack, God provides, and He has everything necessary to create what He has already destined for my life. By the authority of Jesus, I sever every link of past bondage that does not align with His promise.

I declare that I am free, my family is free, and we are victorious and blessed. Ancestral bonds and unfavorable societal trends are nullified in my life and in the lives of my family by the power of the Holy Spirit. I proclaim new freedom, new success, and a new legacy of blessings over myself and future generations.

I decree that my progress will be steady, my success will be assured, and we will move forward from glory to glory, in Jesus' name. Amen.

Reflection:

1. What ancestral bonds or societal trends do you hope to break for your family?

   _____

   _____

   _____

2. What promises has God declared over your life?

   _____

   _____

   _____

"There is peace in the release."

-Latriece M. Spires

Sherna L. Peterson

A Diamond In the Rough

By Sherna L. Peterson

"'For I know the plans that I have for you,' declares the Lord, 'plans for prosperity and not for disaster, to give you a future and a hope.'" (Jeremiah 29:11 NASB)

At eight years old, I kept my gaze on the road as my family's car sped westward, the fields of Mississippi gradually giving way to the rolling plains of Texas. This move symbolized a new beginning. Leaving my friends behind was difficult, but my parents had promised Texas would be full of opportunities. I was a bright and curious girl who loved reading, always excelled in school, and consistently earned good grades. The thought of starting at a new school filled me with both nerves and excitement. Though Texas was where I was born, two years away had made it feel unfamiliar, yet I was ready to face the unknown—just as my parents had taught me.

However, on the first day in my new Texas school, something felt off. Walking confidently into my third-grade classroom with my arms full of school supplies, I greeted the teacher with a wide, friendly smile. The teacher barely acknowledged me and directed me to sit at the back of the room. I didn't think much of it and believed the teacher would warm up to me soon. But as the weeks passed, I noticed I was often overlooked and treated differently from my classmates. My assignments came back with vague comments, and the praise I had grown used to in Mississippi was nowhere to be found.

Then came a devastating shock. One afternoon, I was abruptly informed that I had been placed in the special education program. I didn't fully understand what it meant. The decision had been made behind closed doors, without explanation or my parents' knowledge. I was confused and heartbroken.

My new teacher, Ms. Miller, quickly sensed something was wrong. Kind and patient, Ms. Miller saw that I didn't belong in special education. One day, as she knelt by my desk, she whispered, "Sherna, you're a bright girl. I can see that you understand everything we're doing here. I'm going to talk to your parents about moving you back into your original classroom." Ms. Miller's words were a lifeline. They reassured me that my voice mattered and I wasn't alone.

That evening, my parents met with Ms. Miller. Outraged by the lack of transparency and poor decision-making, they confronted the school administration with an unwavering commitment. After weeks of meetings and paperwork, I was finally removed from the program and returned to my regular classroom. I resumed my studies with renewed determination, though the experience left emotional scars.

I had learned far too early that not everyone recognized my potential as clearly as my family or Ms. Miller did. Yet, my faith became my anchor. I often recalled my grandmother's words, inspired by Psalm 139:14:

"I will give thanks to You, because I am awesomely and wonderfully *made*; Wonderful are Your works, And my soul knows it very well."

As I advanced through school, I encountered both allies and adversaries. By sixth grade, my confidence was blossoming. I maintained strong grades and began helping my classmates with their schoolwork. That year, I achieved a perfect score on an end-of-semester reading exam. Beaming with pride, I handed in my test, feeling on top of the world.

But my teacher's response was crushing. Pulling me aside, she said coldly, "Sherna, you think this score means something? I know you cheated. That's why you'll never amount to anything. One good score doesn't change that. I'm giving you a zero."

I was devastated. I knew I hadn't cheated, yet the teacher's words felt like a heavy weight pressing down on me. As tears streamed down my face, I wanted to disappear. But deep within me, something pushed back. It was as though a still, small voice reminded me of my true worth—not defined by others but rooted in God's truth.

That moment sparked my resolve. I poured myself into my studies and embraced leadership opportunities. I joined the student council, orchestra, track and field, the step team, and various volunteer projects. My teacher's cruel words didn't deter me; they fueled my drive. With God's grace, I became a role model and a young leader, inspiring my peers through my actions and unwavering faith.

High school brought its own challenges but also tremendous growth. With my parents' continued prayers and support, I stayed grounded in my faith. My academic excellence and community involvement earned me a scholarship, making me the first in my family to attend college. I majored in psychology and went on to earn a master's degree.

Even as my career flourished, I felt a persistent tug at my heart—a gentle whisper urging me toward a different path. I tried to push it aside, reassuring myself that I was already making a difference. But the whisper grew stronger, that same still, small voice calling me to go deeper. Finally, after years of resistance, I surrendered my plans to God, praying, "Lord, I'm ready. Show me where You want me to go."

Feeling called to make a difference for children who felt unseen or misunderstood, I embraced my purpose as an educator. I became a distinguished math teacher, renowned for my ability to simplify complex concepts and make them accessible to students of all ages. My classroom became a haven where students not only learned math but also discovered their self-worth and confidence. I reminded them, as I reminded myself, that they were "awesomely and wonderfully made."

Eventually, I transitioned into a role as an instructional coach, mentoring teachers and leaders. I encouraged them to trust God's guidance and use their gifts to uplift others. Looking back, I marveled at how far God had brought me. The trials that had once sought to break me had instead shaped me into a vessel of resilience, encouragement, and hope. My story stood as a testament to God's faithfulness and the power of perseverance.

Prayer:

A Prayer for Women Pursuing Their Calling

Lord, thank You for creating us with purpose and for the plans You have for each of our lives. Help us to hear Your voice clearly, trust Your guidance, and follow the path You have set before us, even when it feels difficult. Give us courage and strength to overcome challenges, and may we be a light to those around us. Teach us to lean not on our own understanding but to trust in You with all our hearts, confident in Your faithfulness to lead us. In Jesus' name. Amen.

Reflection:

1. What obstacles have you faced that could have held you back, and how has your faith empowered you to overcome them?

   _____

   _____

   _____

2. How have you witnessed God working through difficult situations in your life, turning them into opportunities for good?

   _____

   _____

   _____

3. What practical steps can you take to better hear and follow God's guidance in your career or personal life?

   _____

   _____

   _____

> "I once feared being unmarried at 40.
> Now I'm more concerned with being married to the
> wrong person in my 40's."
>
> —Latriece M. Spires

Dr. Kimberlee D. Bassa

When You Just Don't Know What to Do

By Dr. Kimberlee D. Bassa

"In you, Lord my God, I put my trust." (Psalms 25:1 NIV)

"Trust in the Lord with all your heart and lean not on your own understanding." (Proverbs 3:5 NIV)

There you are—stuck, confused, and frustrated. You just don't know what to do, which way to turn, or even if you need to turn at all. What's next? What do you do? There's the question: "What do you do when you just don't know what to do?" In this age of technology, I decided to ask Google and ChatGPT that very question, and I must admit, both platforms provided what seemed like sound advice. Suggestions such as stepping back to reflect, journaling, and asking for perspectives were among the guidance given. And yes, those are definitely action steps that could assist in gaining clarity and direction. However, as I have journeyed through life, I have found that trusting in my Savior is, bar none, the most reliable move to make when I just don't know what to do.

I come from a God-fearing family. Raised in the church, there was no doubt that each Sunday, Tuesday, and any other day there was a program or church-related event, we were in attendance. I watched my grandparents and my mother praise and serve the Lord. So, trusting in Him and His Word was ingrained in me. In my heart, mind, and soul, I believed trusting the Lord was my response to everything—or so I thought. When the day came that I began to struggle with trusting the Lord, I was shaken to my core. I couldn't believe that I was questioning Him—His timing, His plan, and His love. I questioned it all. Honestly, my "homegrown" trust in my Father in Heaven was fading. I even wondered if my trust in God had ever been real.

Many of us have heard this famous phrase: "You have your good days and your bad days." Well, I'd had some good days, but it seemed the bad days were winning. It was a time in my life when day after day, month after month, and yes, year after year, circumstances and unfortunate events seemed to be boxed, gift-wrapped, and delivered to my front door daily. I began to feel as if there was a sign on my back that read, "Here, get Kim." I felt like nothing could go right. No matter how much I read or prayed, nothing was going well. It was then that I made the decision to lean on my own understanding.

I remember being in my room, frustrated, crying, and mad. I decided to take matters into my own hands. After all, I knew what I wanted and what I needed. From that point on, I began writing my own plan, and I did just that. I changed everything. Now, keep in mind, I grew up in church, so I kept on praying. I just told God what I wanted and how I wanted Him to bless my plan. He was my Savior, but didn't He promise to grant me the desires of my heart? I continued on my own path to greatness. There wasn't anything that I couldn't do. I enrolled in school, started dating someone new, got a new job, started hanging out with new friends, and even added two new ministries to my plan. I was connected, serving, working, and yet, nothing had changed. Things still weren't going well. In fact, I was emptier, unfulfilled, and even angrier with the Lord. Why aren't you answering me? Why haven't you changed my situation?

"Trust me," He said. "Why?" I asked. I *had* trusted Him, and was still miserable. I didn't know what to do. I had tried everything. It had come to a point where everything was a facade. I was on the stage of "fake it until you make it" everywhere I went and in everything I did. Crying had become a part of my nightly routine, and going through the motions was my means of getting through the day. I didn't want to talk to anyone about my situation because no one could know that my faith was fading and my trust in God was next to none. If I told my family, they would say, "Pray and trust in the Lord." If I told my friends, they would ask if I had prayed about it. And truthfully, praying and trusting in the Lord to heal my situation was the last thing I wanted to hear. He didn't come through–or grant me the desires of my heart.

One morning, oddly enough, I woke up a little after two o'clock. My heart was heavy. My mind was overloaded with all of my "whys" and "why nots." I sat up on the side of the bed and cried uncontrollably. I was at my breaking point. I laid face down on the floor and cried, but this was not a regular cry. This was the cry that shouted out to the Lord. It was the cry that shifted me from "homegrown" to my own trust in the Lord. Again, God told me to trust Him, and this time I asked Him, "How? How do I trust You?" He said, "Get to know Me." I was confused because I *thought* I knew the Lord. We had a relationship. I went to church. I served. I knew Him. But the question was, did I know Him for myself? Had I been coasting on my grandparents' and my mother's relationships with the Lord? Did I truly know the Lord and trust Him for myself?

Trustworthy relationships are crafted when intentional time is spent getting to know one another. The difference in our relationship with the Lord is that He already knows us. He wants us to spend time with Him so we can know Him for ourselves and craft a relationship rooted in faith, belief, and trust. For a long time, I didn't know what to do. I was hurt, lost, and struggled to trust in the Lord. But when I decided to know the Lord for myself, my relationship with Him began to grow its own roots.

Spending time with the Lord and knowing Him for myself allows my trust in Him to be the firm foundation I need when I am stuck and unsure of what to do. Trusting in Him with all my heart is a direct result of truly knowing Him. This trust is the most reliable navigation system for my life. It gives me the directions I need right when I need them. As I continue on my life journey, I still have times when I just don't know what to do, but I stand on His Word in Psalms 25:1: "In you, Lord my God, I put my trust." When I trust Him, my actions align with His Word, and I can move forward even when it feels like I just don't know what to do.

Prayer:

Lord, let my trust in You be the roots of my soul, grounding me in Your love and wisdom. May Your Word be the compass that guides my steps, aligning me with the path You've set before me. When I feel lost and my way is unclear, remind me that trusting You fully means surrendering all my doubts, fears and plans. Help me place my faith in You at every moment, knowing that You are ever-present to love, guide, and protect me. Let my trust in You be steadfast and unwavering. In the guiding Name of Jesus. Amen.

Reflection:

1. In what areas of your life do you need to align your actions more closely with God's Word to fully place your trust in Him?

   _____

   _____

   _____

2. When facing challenges, how do you draw closer to your Heavenly Father to rely on His promises and strengthen your trust in His Word?

   _____

   _____

   _____

Latriece M. Spires

Pass Me the Fig Leaves Please

By Latriece M. Spires

"Then the eyes of both of them were opened, and they realized they were naked; so they sewed fig leaves together and made coverings for themselves." (Genesis 3:7 NIV)

"She gave this name to the Lord who spoke to her: 'You are the God who sees me,' for she said, 'I have now seen the One who sees me.'" (Genesis 16:13 NIV)

The Wild, Wild West -AKA- The Dating Scene

As I walked into the cozy little tea shop, there he was, standing with his massive, muscular arms stretched wide. Chile, it felt like a scene straight out of a movie. *Picture that moment in Pretty Woman where Richard Gere is on the fire escape with flowers in one hand, arms wide open.* When I finally reached his table, he grabbed me and literally swept me off my feet—lifting *all* of my plus-size pounds into the air. I felt as light as the sweet cream foam floating at the top of my favorite tea. My feet were dangling! I'd never experienced anything like that before.

This wasn't our first meeting, but I must admit, it felt like it was. I instantly melted into the arms of this beautiful, 6'4" specimen of a man. Honey, if we were a s'more, then I was definitely the gooey center.

"You're perfect," he said.

I looked around to see who he could possibly be talking to.

"Perfect? Who, me? Couldn't be!"

The truth is, I knew I was anything but perfect. Yet, he looked right at me and said, "Latriece, you are perfect. When I saw you, I saw my future."

As we continued getting to know each other, an opportunity arose to have a real, uncomfortable conversation. Turns out, he had a few other "situations," and it was time to unpack his roster. I asked questions to gain clarity because I needed to know what his goals were. I also shared my own perspective and goals.

And just like that (snaps fingers), my version of a fairytale ended. Shortly after, I realized that "perfection" comes with a hefty price. Remember Job? He was blameless, upright, and feared the Lord (Job 1:1). Yet even Job wasn't exempt from trials.

Sis, have you ever been so exhausted that not just your mind and body were tired, but even your *tears* felt tired? I'm talking about the kind of fatigue where your tears seem to have a soul of their own—weary, worn, and single. That right eye stays ready to drop a tear at any moment. That's the type of weariness I've experienced in this new world of dating.

I know the Lord sees me, but at times I don't want Him to. As folks like to say, "Life be lifing," and I haven't always made the best choices. Even now, my stomach twists at the thought of another failed relationship. The cycle has been vicious, and the exhaustion is real.

Take, for instance, another gentleman I met unexpectedly. We dated, decided to make it official, and before I knew it, I rang in the new year with someone who wouldn't even make it to spring. The red flags were subtle but present, and there's only so much ignoring you can do. Maybe I tolerated his brokenness because I hadn't yet dealt with my own.

I know I was created to be a helper, but first, I needed to help myself. So many women share this story—we stumble, we fall, and some of us have yet to get back up. But here's where my story differs: my mother.

She doesn't let me wallow in failure. For her, getting back up isn't *an* option—it's *the* option. "Get up and swing a little harder next time," she always says. By now, I know her pep talks by heart. I also know her encouragement comes from her own unspoken experiences.

> *When he finds me, it's not that I'll remove my mother as my emergency contact, but I'll add him. You see, I'm already living a full life. Any person I add at this point has to add value. My perspective has changed, so my actions have changed. – Latriece M. Spires*

Through my hurts, I'm learning to harvest. I call it "harvesting from my hurts." The lessons I've gained from discomfort have been invaluable. I've learned to fight fair—even in my fatigue—because some relationships are worth it. But I've also learned to reserve my energy for the right people.

Your best effort will never be good enough for the wrong ones. I've spent too much time being an option for people I placed high on my priority list. And I'm not just talking about men—I'm talking about those other "ships," too. You know, the one-sided friendships that yield little to no fruit.

I've released the weight of trying to be everything for everybody, only to end up with a treasure box full of dust in return. I had to have a real "come-to-Jesus meeting" with myself: "Why are you fighting so hard for relationships that don't serve you?" After all, I matter, too. I'm no longer willing to overlook my well-being to pacify someone else.

8 Toes In, Pinky Toes Out

2 Chronicles 7:13-16; Esther 4:14

I've recently decided to stop trying to do things my way. Nah, sis, I'm good on that bottomless abyss of nothingness! Time and time again, I've made the decision to make it happen—with or without Him. I'm ashamed to admit that, but then again, maybe my truth will set another sister free. Maybe I was created for a time such as this.

What if I've been the reason for my own delay?

I was indeed eight toes in, with my pinky toes out. I wasn't fully committed. Sure, I made Him my Savior years ago, but only recently did I decide to make Him my Lord. That means I'm choosing to trust Him—with everything, everyone, and every situation—in His way and His timing.

Now, don't get it twisted, beloved—I'm still figuring it all out, just like you. My journey has been anything but linear. I'm in the process of cultivating an environment big enough for the person I am growing into.

In *Atomic Habits*, James Clear wrote something that has stuck with me: "And I knew that if things were going to improve, I was the one responsible for making it happen." That hit me. The little girl in me is excited about this seasoned version of myself. I've finally entered the era of keeping commitments to myself.

> *And then there was Jesus, my Savior. I owe Him EVERYTHING! He is so kind. When I run to the fig leaves to cover my shame, He reminds me to run to Him—the forgiver of all my sins. The way He pieces me back together so intricately is beautiful. He speaks to my heart and reminds me I'm His. – Latriece M. Spires*

Nannie B. and Me

John 5: 1-10

Allowing myself time to grieve has been one of the most healing things I've ever done. Every day looks different, and I'm okay with that. I've come to realize there's a space in my life that can't be filled by anything or anyone else.

The truth is, my grandmother physically left this earth in July 2021, but pieces of her drifted away bit by bit long before then. Watching the strongest, most independent, kindest, and most selfless woman I knew be reduced to complete dependence—in every way—was gut-wrenching. It's messed up, and it hurts—STILL.

Even though I don't understand why, I'm at peace with what the Lord allowed. In her final days, as she prepared to enter her place of rest, she NEVER stopped praising. If she didn't recognize or understand anything else, she still feared the Lord. That was a sight to see: her worshipping and praising even in her last moments.

What an AWESOME GOD she served—we serve!

I can still see her hands stretched high, as if reaching for the highest heaven, swaying gently to the tunes of Lee Williams, Sam Cooke, or Debra Snipes. It was pure joy to witness. Oh, how I miss her. I long to kiss her again, to feel the ripples of her soft, crinkly skin resting so beautifully against mine. Her smile, her laugh, her jokes—they were immeasurable!

As I continue to give myself permission to heal, I can see the Lord's handiwork in every step of this journey. Even though the pain lingers at times, I feel a peace that is truly indescribable. I choose to take up my bed and meet Jesus at the pool as many times as I need to so that I can be made well.

Allow Me to Reintroduce Myself

Isaiah 43:19 NIV

I'm no longer that fragile child of God I once was. That title, as of late, just doesn't fit. I am the grateful daughter of King Jesus. I'm a servant leader, ministry leader, educational leader, author, coach, consultant, business owner, ministry founder, and a future full-time entrepreneur. I'm also a daughter, sister, aunt, niece, cousin, friend, Godmom, and soon-to-be wife to my earthly king!

I live an incredibly full life, and I'm so grateful for those I get to share it with. Let me be clear: none of these roles have been accomplished in my own strength. I take no credit. It is the Lord who has given me the privilege to serve His people in each of these capacities. Fasting and praying have become consistent parts of my walk with Christ, and they've been essential in shaping me for this journey.

As I mature in my faith, I'm starting to see the beauty in peace and simplicity. I've always been a high-achiever, but these days, I'm seeking something even more valuable: time, experiences, and the people I love to share them with.

Though my community may be small, it's pretty amazing. A big thank you to Jennie Allen's Find Your People for helping me redefine the spaces I create. At this stage in life, anyone I invite into my circle cannot be a taker only. Reciprocation is paramount! Why? Because I'm the kind of friend who will climb to the rooftop and lower you into the house so you can have your personal encounter with Jesus. I now expect the same level of intentionality from the people in my community. That's all I have space for right now—true, authentic relationships.

Prayer:

Oh Lord, You are great and greatly to be praised! There is none like You. You, oh God, know every detail about us—from the crown of our heads to the soles of our feet. You are sovereign! I thank You, God, for loving us and keeping us. I thank You for the different life experiences because we know that each story can be used for Your glory. Please forgive our sins, Father.

I pray for every heart that reads this chapter. I ask that Your strength be perfected in their times of fatigue and weakness. Replenish their souls as often as they need it. Grant peace in their hearts, peace in their minds, peace at home, peace at work, and peace at their places of worship.

I pray that when weapons are formed against them, they are crushed at the mention of Your name. Finally, I pray for their belief and hope in You to be unwavering—that they will trust in Your promises and seek Your Kingdom and righteousness first, knowing that all other things will be added, as Your word promises.

In the Mighty, Matchless name of Jesus the Christ, I pray. Amen.

Reflection:

1. What areas of your life have you not yet fully surrendered to God?

   _____

   _____

   _____

2. What does total submission to Christ look like for you?

   _____

   _____

   _____

Meet The Authors

Aveia Jones is an active member of Rockwall Friendship Baptist Church, where she serves in the Stephen Ministry. This ministry is dedicated to providing high-quality, one-to-one, Christ-centered care to individuals facing life challenges. Stephen Ministry offers long-term care and support, walking alongside individuals during difficult times. Professionally, Aveia is a commercial real estate professional, a licensed Texas Real Estate Broker, and an aspiring real estate developer. She holds a Bachelor of Business Administration from the University of Texas at Austin, where she studied Architectural Engineering and Business Administration through the McCombs School of Business.

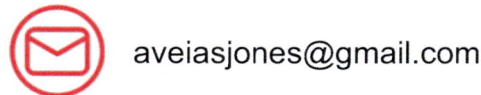 aveiasjones@gmail.com

Brandi Epps, a Dallas native, is a multifaceted professional with a wealth of experience and talent. She has dedicated 16 years to education, where she excels as a passionate and accomplished educator. Outside of her career, Brandi is a mother, ministry leader, doctoral candidate, podcaster, author, and speaker. Her unwavering faith in God, combined with her experiences in urban classrooms, personal relationships, and life challenges, equips her to inspire purpose, passion, encouragement, hope, and confidence in those she encounters. She firmly believes that God has blessed her with a unique gift for transforming the lives and hearts of children, teachers, young adults, and women.

 www.brandiwholeheartedly.com

 @brandi_wholeheartedly

Chrisdya S. Houston, M. Ed. a proud Dallas native, believes that "the sky does not have to be your limit when it can be your launching pad." After completing her education at Dallas ISD, she graduated from Southern Methodist University with degrees in Journalism, Psychology, and Sociology. She later earned a Master of Education from the University of Texas at Arlington. Chrisdya currently works as a Dyslexia Interventionist and owns a boutique travel agency and marketing firm. In her free time, she enjoys spending quality time with family and friends, reading, and traveling.

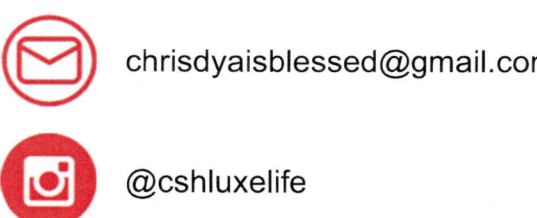

chrisdyaisblessed@gmail.com

@cshluxelife

Christin Burton, a native of Buffalo, New York, currently works as an LPN Supervisor with Neighborhood Health Center, serving the inner-city community of Buffalo. She is also a devoted mother to two daughters. In addition to her professional career, Christin is the owner and host of the up-and-coming podcast *Get Out of Dodge*. The podcast focuses on healing, her personal spiritual journey as a pastor's daughter, and meaningful discussions about societal and generational issues.

🌐 www.getoutdodge.com

👍 getoutofdodge

📷 @getoutofdodge97

Dr. Kathlyn "Dr. Kat" Spires Diaz is an accomplished educator, second language acquisition specialist, bilingual case manager, mother, grandmother, and devoted child of God. She currently works in the public sector, overseeing six school districts in Multnomah County, Oregon. In her role, she assists at-risk high school students and their families by helping them navigate various programs and services. As an African American, culturally specific case manager, Dr. Kat is deeply passionate about advocating for her students, helping them build social capital, and encouraging them to reach their full potential. Outside of work, she enjoys spending quality time with her mother, siblings, son, and two grandchildren.

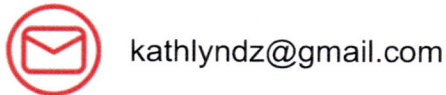 kathlyndz@gmail.com

Dr. Katina Briscoe, born in Searcy, Arkansas, and raised in Augusta, Arkansas, is a dedicated family nurse practitioner and geriatric clinical nurse specialist. She has devoted her life to providing compassionate care and is passionate about serving her community. Dr. Briscoe is also a wife, mother, grandmother, speaker, and author. A member of the Church of God in Christ in Augusta AR, she teaches Sunday School weekly. In addition to her professional and community commitments, Dr. Briscoe is an active member of Zeta Phi Beta Sorority, Inc., and enjoys reading, music, and playing the trumpet.

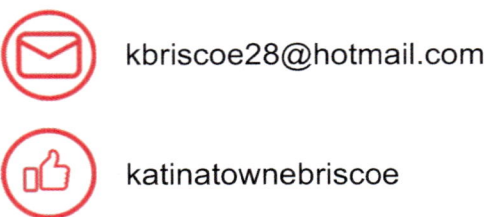

kbriscoe28@hotmail.com

katinatownebriscoe

Meet The Authors

Dr. Kimberlee D. Bassa is a passionate educator dedicated to providing enriched and equitable opportunities for all students. She finds immense joy in spending time with her family, especially her five nieces, who bring laughter and happiness into her life. In her free time, she enjoys staying active, traveling, and listening to music. Guided by the principles of prayer, consistency, and simplicity, Dr. Bassa remains grounded and connected in both her personal and professional life.

 kbassa3@gmail.com

Ebony Alexandra, a native of Buffalo, NY, and currently residing in Dallas, TX, is the visionary behind Her Obsession Brand, which is dedicated to empowering and supporting women. She is also the founder of Opulent Business Solutions, an accounting firm in Dallas. Ebony is deeply committed to uplifting women, values her large family, and embraces her role as a dog mom. As a devoted believer in Christ, she is guided by her faith and driven by a passion for making a meaningful impact in the lives of others.

 msejones11@gmail.com

Meet The Authors

Latriece M. Spires is a devoted follower of Jesus Christ and a committed servant leader. Born in Oakland, California, and raised in the small community of Marvell, Arkansas, she currently holds leadership roles in various areas of her life. Latriece is the author of three children's books and a co-author of two anthologies, accomplishments she attributes to God's grace. In addition, she leads her own ministry, The Matters of Her Heart, through which she ministers to and uplifts fellow sisters in Christ. Latriece cherishes her roles as a daughter, sister, aunt, niece, cousin, friend, god-mom, and is joyfully preparing to become the wife of her earthly king.

 www.syscoachingandconsulting.com

 @herheartflow

 @syscoachingandconsulting

Leondra Williams, a native of Pine Bluff, Arkansas, has dedicated her entire career to the field of education. Her professional journey includes roles as a classroom teacher, literacy coach, principal, and National Board Certified Educator, all within her community. She is a recent graduate of Arkansas State University, where she earned an Educational Specialist degree in Superintendency. Leondra is an active member of True Vine E.M.B.C. and the proud mother of three children. Her children are her greatest inspiration, motivating her to pursue excellence and ensuring that every action she takes is meaningful and impactful.

 leondrawilliams2024@gmail.com

 leondra.williams.2024

Meet The Authors

Satavia Hazley Austin, MBA, RN, CHPO, is the Principal CEO of Star of Texas Hospice. Satavia is an industry trailblazer, leading one of the few Black-owned hospices in the country. Star of Texas Hospice has served thousands of patients at the end of life. A Magna Cum Laude graduate of Houston Baptist University, her passion for community outreach began during her time there as a charter member of Alpha Kappa Alpha Sorority, Inc. She also holds an MBA from LeTourneau University. Satavia attributes her success to God and the unwavering support of her husband, two sons, and her parents.

www.sataviaaustin.com

sataviahazleyaustin

@sataviaaustin

Sherna L. Peterson, a native of Dallas, Texas, is the owner of Life Essence Transformational Coaching. Through her coaching practice, she empowers clients to gain a deeper understanding of their goals and develop actionable plans to achieve their desired outcomes. Sherna is also a proud mother to one daughter. With 18 years of experience in education, she currently serves as a Lead Instructional Coach in the second-largest school district in Texas, where she continues to inspire growth and excellence.

leilani7769@gmail.com

shernalp

@thebeautyof_sherna

Made in the USA
Coppell, TX
20 May 2025

49409685R00079